The Options Doctor

Founded in 1807, John Wiley & Sons is the oldest independent publishing company in the United States. With offices in North America, Europe, Australia, and Asia, Wiley is globally committed to developing and marketing print and electronic products and services for our customers' professional and personal knowledge and understanding.

The Wiley Trading series features books by traders who have survived the market's ever changing temperament and have prospered—some by reinventing systems, others by getting back to basics. Whether a novice trader, professional, or somewhere in-between, these books will provide the advice and strategies needed to prosper today and well into the future.

For a list of available titles, visit our web site at www.WileyFinance.com.

The Options Doctor

Option Strategies
for Every Kind
of Market

JEANETTE SCHWARZ YOUNG

John Wiley & Sons, Inc.

Published by John Wiley & Sons, Inc., Hoboken, New Jersey.
Published simultaneously in Canada.

Illustrations courtesy of Lisa Mareiniss Rutledge, www.lisamareinissrutledge.com.

For general information on our other products and services or for technical
support, please contact our Customer Care Department within the
United States at (800) 762-2974, outside the United States at (317) 572-3993
or fax (317) 572-4002.

Wiley also publishes its books in a variety of electronic formats. Some content
that appears in print may not be available in electronic books. For more
information about Wiley products, visit our web site at www.wiley.com.

Library of Congress Cataloging-in-Publication Data:

Young, Jeanette Schwarz, 1944–
    The options doctor : option strategies for every kind of market / Jeanette
Schwarz Young.
        p.   cm.—(Wiley trading series)
    Includes index.
    ISBN-13 978-0-471-77772-4 (cloth)
    ISBN-10 0-471-77772-2 (cloth)
    1. Options (Finance).   2. Investment analysis.   I. Title.
HG6024.A3Y68   2007
332.64'53—dc22

                                                            2006029336

Printed in the United States of America.

10   9   8   7   6   5   4   3   2   1

This book is dedicated to the survivors of 9/11, both in New York and in Washington, DC. We at the New York Board of Trade (NYBOT) work at the only exchange that was demolished by this terrorist act. While we are the lucky ones, many of us suffered from this horror visited to our home away from home, so this is for those who live with the memory of that awful day.

Contents

Preface   ix

Acknowledgments   xv

About the Author   xvii

PART I   Market Outlook   1

CHAPTER 1   What Is Technical Analysis?   3

CHAPTER 2   Basic Charting   19

CHAPTER 3   Identifying Trends and Calculating
             Support and Resistance   43

CHAPTER 4   Pattern Recognition   59

CHAPTER 5   Momentum and Other Indicators   83

CHAPTER 6   Bonds, Currencies,
             and Commodities   91

PART II   Options Strategies   107

CHAPTER 7   Introduction to Options   109

CHAPTER 8   Using Options in Trending Markets   129

CHAPTER 9   Using Options in Trading
             Range Markets   139

CHAPTER 10   Using Options in Reversing Markets   153

PART III   Managing a Position   **165**

CHAPTER 11 Fundamental Hedging Strategies   **167**

CHAPTER 12 Managing a Losing Position   **177**

CHAPTER 13 Managing a Winning Position   **189**

CHAPTER 14 Pulling It All Together   **195**

APPENDIX   Trading Tools I Have Developed   **207**

Index   **211**

Preface

I'll never forget the first day I heard of the New York Futures Exchange (NYFE). I was a broker for Thomson McKinnon Securities in Morristown, New Jersey. Our office was visited by two representatives of the NYFE. I was the syndicate coordinator for that branch office and held a commodities license (Series 3) as well as the ordinary Series 7 (general securities), along with several other licenses. The very idea of futures was scary! My office was immediately adjacent to an active commodities broker's office at the branch. Generally, all you could hear from the room was the racket emanating from the squawk box carrying the transactions from the floor of the NYFE. Little did I know then that my career was unfolding before me.

I had become a broker in March of 1981. I was hired in January, took the exam, and passed it. That was the requisite introductory education afforded me by the firm. I was one of two rookies in the board room, and I must admit that I knew less than my fellow rookie George, who at least had a business background. My background was that of an amateur stock picker.

I recall vividly the day I received that phone call telling me that I had passed the Series 7. Our branch manager, Mike, told me I had passed and to start selling, now! Selling what? And to whom? These questions were not answered. The guy sitting behind me was an old German who religiously ate garlic at breakfast and seemed to have a stock or two to sell. I asked him for guidance and he told me to "sell Mobot." I asked what it was and was informed that it was a company that built industrial robots. That sounded good, so off I went, dialing for dollars, trying to sell Mobot. That was when I learned the value of research.

I approached the firm's syndicate guy for a hot stock for those of my customers who were also customers of DH Blair. As you might remember, that company always had hot stocks. It appeared that they would "pump and dump," but if you were good and promised to buy the dogs, you'd get the winners, too. I requested a hot stock and was asked if I was kidding—no, of course, not. I had to compete, and everything I showed my clients was boring, dull, and went nowhere! Welcome to Wall Street! My firm was so stodgy that when I brought them a possible initial public offering (IPO) in a cellular telephone company, they asked for five years of financials. Five years of financials!?! The whole idea was new and nobody had five years of financials.

The radio spectrum was being divided (allocated) and sold to little mom-and-pop phone companies. This was during the time when the Federal Communications Commission (FCC) in its infinite wisdom decided to make the radio spectrum available to smaller companies so that AT&T could not dominate the spectrum. Small phone companies could bid on the spectrum and were awarded their pieces of the pie, along with AT&T. The cellular telephone company in question had contracted with many of these little phone companies and went to bid on the spectrum. It ended up with a capability to provide cellular service to compete with AT&T. This was in the era made memorable by Judge Greene's divestiture ruling against AT&T. So my firm, Thomson McKinnon, missed out on US Cellular. Where are cell phones now? Where is AT&T? A mandatory, regulated preclusion against earning more than their 7 percent per annum wasn't enough? Then there was the cubic zirconium company I brought to them; well, that is yet another story. That company is still in business today, without having gone public.

Today I am a floor broker/trader/hedger/strategist on the floor at the New York Board of Trade. To give you an idea of my world, try to recall high school. Remember the class clown, who invariably was a smart, bored kid with more energy than could be dealt with? Visualize 500 class clowns, all in a room together! Add in the smells and sounds of a men's locker room and you'll begin to get an idea of the world of a floor broker.

WHY I WROTE THIS BOOK

So what does this have to do with technical analysis and options? I thought that I was pretty savvy before I entered this world, a world that has the ability to humble the most arrogant person. I had a knowledge base from which to work, but the experience and practical knowledge acquired on the floor is incredible.

This knowledge, which I will share, changed both the way I trade and the way I think. It has also, inevitably, made me a bit louder and pushier. Next to the others whom I trade with, I am a pussycat, quiet and nonemotional. To be a good trader, you must check your ego at the door. As a recovered divorcée, my ego had long before been removed; being a floor trader eradicated any remaining traces. The market has no emotions and cares not one whit whether you are right or wrong. On the one hand, it is cold, cruel, and uncaring. On the other hand, it can be both stimulating and fascinating.

Options have been viewed by most as very difficult to use and impossible to understand. Not so; this subject is easily understood. The difficulty arises from some of the terminology rather than the meaning of those terms. I have written this book in very plain English so that even a novice can understand what I am talking about, even though of the strategies are intricate.

It is my goal to make you an options-friendly creature, so you can eventually enjoy using these investment tools to enhance your trading. I hope you find the book user-friendly and that you enjoy the lessons and feel as though you can, at the very least, understand some of the options lingo and strategies. Along the way, I am showing you another way to increase your income and improve your imagination. Have fun with the book; I know I had fun writing it.

HOW THIS BOOK IS ORGANIZED

The first thing you need to know is how to understand the market. There are different approaches to this; mine is a marriage between technical analysis and fundamental analysis. As a technical analyst, I rely heavily on my charts and figures. It is also important that the companies you are looking at make economic sense (for the bulls) or are really full of hot air (for the bears). Thus, you must look at the fundamentals of a company. I like companies that make money, pay dividends, and have insider ownership with good growth and a price-earnings (P/E) ratio that is relatively low. Those are my rules and I rarely stray far from them. There will be a lot of companies that qualify, and that is where technical analysis comes into the picture. Why opt for an issue that has a bad chart pattern? This analysis technique allows you to see visually where the company is and where it might be going.

In the first part of this book I show you how to use some tools to aid you in your research. As a commodities trader, charts tell you everything you need to know about a commodity. Most commodities traders are closet chartists, anyway. Commodities tend to chart really well.

The remainder of this book teaches you some basics about options and about hedging, and invites you to use your newfound knowledge in up markets, down markets, trending markets, trading range markets, losing positions, and winning positions. Hopefully, your imagination will be fed enough for you to think about things not mentioned in this book.

The Options Doctor is in.

A FINAL WORD BEFORE YOU BEGIN

Recently, one of my repair strategies was used by a newcomer to trading. This ended in disaster. Why? Because he did not thoroughly understand options and their consequences. This poor soul was looking for a quick fix to a very bad investment decision. He had shorted the market and watched as the position moved against him. It wasn't until the position was out of control that he looked for possible solutions to the problem. Obviously, he never heard of a stop-loss limit order. It seemed as though he was frozen in his spot and just watched his money and the trade go against him. Then, when he sought advice, he did not admit to his lack of knowledge about options. This led to a fix that would have worked had he left it alone. The initial advice and secondary advice were ignored; the strategy was partially implemented and the delta was trashed. He mangled the position by overselling some of the options and then covering his short, putting him at further risk. It was a mess.

You may not yet understand all of the intricacies of this story, but by the end of the book you will. The moral is this: If you want to try some of these strategies, be sure you first understand what you are doing. Don't try to tell the market what you want it to do; it's better to let the market tell you what to do. Caution should always be taken and you should understand that a so-called quick fix can take months to work out. Some of the repairs will take months to adjust, but time will heal the mess. Most errors should be reversed and removed without options, but if you are going to use options you need to understand what you are doing and always take the conservative road.

Here I am, the Options Doctor. Comfortable shoes are a must on the trading floor because we are on our feet all day, so you'll see I'm wearing my Uggs. The doors to my office are open, so read on.

JEANETTE SCHWARZ YOUNG

Acknowledgments

Some books write themselves. Although such an experience has been limited in this effort, honesty obliges me to acknowledge the impacts upon my career of the overarching competencies of others with whom I was privileged to be acquainted and career-involved.

I first met Jack Solomon upon joining Thomson McKinnon Securities in 1981. He gave me my commitment to technical analysis, a competence he possessed, exercised, and shared with me. As a cub broker in 1981, I entered the board room in a period of market retreat, with skyrocketing interest rates and tumbling real estate values. We had lines at the gas pumps and a U.S. dollar with the dubious status of being one peg above trash. Jimmy Carter had just been defeated by Ronald Reagan. The time was not the best; it was nearly impossible for brokers, let alone women brokers. I can unfondly recall one official telling me to go home and have kids; my answer was: "Did that; now, I have to support them." He just glared at me in response.

I had the good fortune to meet a man during those difficult days who would thereafter become my mentor in technical analysis. He taught me technologies that are not yet available in print. In those days, our tools solely comprised the *Wall Street Journal* and the blue and green chart books, called *Daily Graphs*, which were delivered to our office by Monday morning's opening. Our tools were a ruler and a No. 3 pencil. This, in truth, is how it all started.

Further acknowledgments must go to John Murphy, whose writings have largely provided the backbone to technical analysis. His unique ability to communicate and to explain intermarket relationships is fundamental to the bible of our discipline.

To this list, I must gratefully include the man who has been there for me, a friend and mentor to my writing. Joseph Chislow has been a lifelong friend, always available, always willing to help me with the writing and the editing of my work.

Lisa Mareiniss Rutledge (www.lisamareinissrutledge.com) has contributed her talents as the illustrator. She is a classically trained artist who has created artwork and murals in private homes and businesses and has contributed to a number of shared art shows in and around New York City. Thank you Lisa for all your hard work on this project and for making this book something special.

Then there are all the people who wrote the books that I studied. That list is far too long for me to name all of them, but their contributions to the competencies that I hope to convey to you, the reader, are what make this effort possible.

Finally, "thanks" is but a feeble word to express to my father, who, distressed at my obvious stage fright in piano performances, shoved me into the market at the tender age of 12, kicking and screaming all the way; thank you, Dr. Dad, for giving me the love for the excitement of the market.

J. S. Y.

About the Author

Jeanette Schwarz Young, CFP, CMT, earned her bachelor's and master's degrees at Adelphi University. As a member of the New York Board of Trade (NYBOT), she is an active member of the floor, options settlement, membership, and members benefit committees. She began her career in the brokerage business in 1981 with Thomson McKinnon Securities, where, under the guidance of Jack Solomon, she honed her skills as a technical analyst. Since starting her career, Ms. Young has obtained 10 National Association of Securities Dealers (NASD) licenses.

Ms. Young has earned acclaim from her peers for her demonstrated technical and technician capabilities. Her experience runs the gamut from floor executions to hedging and extends to the back office (having run a self-clearing firm). Today, she is known as a financial writer and as a strategist-technician. Her market letter, "The Option Queen Letter," has been published in *Barron's*, and her article "Managing Risk with Options" was a front-page feature in *The CRB Trader*. Another featured article, entitled "The Commodities Channel Index Revisited," appeared in *Technical Analysis of Stocks and Commodities* magazine. She also wrote "Lessons from the Trading Floor: Strategies Anyone Can Use," published in the June 2005 issue of *SFO* magazine. You may have seen her on several live and taped Fox News, CNN-fn, Bloomberg, and CNBC broadcasts. She can also be seen on NYBOT-TV (www.nybot.com), where she broadcasts a daily financial news report.

Ms. Young is an appointed member of the President's Advisory Council of Adelphi University. She is a member of numerous financial organizations, including the FPA, AAPTA, and MTA. She received a top 10 winner award in the National Investment Challenge, Pro Options Division, for two years and has even placed in the top three in the world. Ms. Young is included in *Trader Monthly's* "Women in Trading" celebration, published in the October/November 2006 issue. She was also a recently featured trader in *Forbes* magazine.

The
Options
Doctor

PART I

Market Outlook

The bull/bear represents the market, which is never stagnant. It is either too happy or too sad. Possibly the market has a dual personality, that of a bull and that of a bear. Most of the time the market suffers from bipolar disease and is never medicated. The purpose of Part I is to learn how to solve for the personality of the market by the use of the various technical tools. The bull/bear represents this goal.

Bull and bear.

Chapter 1 tells you about technical analysis and gives you some basic background on this discipline. Chapter 2 shows you how to chart and the many different ways the same numbers can be plotted. By Chapter 3, you are ready to identify trends and solve for direction, identifying both support and resistance levels. Chapter 4 simply discusses pattern recognition and what you might expect as a result of various patterns. Chapter 5 is another tool in your trading toolbox that equips you with more knowledge. The final chapter in this part looks at important asset classes: bonds, currencies, and commodities.

CHAPTER 1

What Is Technical Analysis?

The day Henry Ford rolled his first jalopy off a Michigan assembly line is forever marked in our calendars as the last day knowing stockholders maintained shares positions in the buggy-whip business. Was it the last day to unload? Were there other days better suited to recoverable investment disposition? What were the indicators? This is the stuff on which success or failure in volatile markets is based. To answer predictive concerns, the canny investor must turn to sources more reliable than necromancy, fortune-telling, crystal balls, and tarot cards (although we have no objection to any reliable outside help in our endeavors). It is from this unsatisfied concern that technical analysis was developed.

So, what then *is* technical analysis? How can it help me with my business? These are the primary questions any canny investor asks when first exposed to the art of technical analysis. (Yes, I said the *art* of technical analysis. Specifically, space visualization skills are necessary for mastering this form of analysis.) Technical analysts believe all information about the subject of analysis is reflected in the visual presentation of the trading in that issue. That visual presentation is called a chart or a graph. What this graph reflects are all the trades that occurred in that issue in the designated time period of study. The price that you can see visually reflects all information about the issue, both public and private. The technical analyst believes that this information reflects the fundamentals of the issue and all inside and public information about that issue.

Technical analysis can be used to develop asset allocation models, which identify the more favorable sectors to the exclusion of the weaker ones. What do we mean by that? If, let us say, the semiconductors are weak and gold is strong; that difference will show on a chart. You would look at the gold index (XAU) and compare it to the semiconductor index (SOX) for a general glance, as a comparison. Does that mean we should sell our semiconductor stocks? Hardly! Rather, what it tells us is that we need to understand where support and resistance lie, so that we can fine-tune our allocation models. It could well be that semiconductors are a buy and gold is running into resistance. These tools that we are going to learn to use will help us to model our portfolios in a more efficient and optimal way, using support, resistance, and other measures to keep our profits running and our losses at a minimum.

You do not need complicated programs to begin this study—just graph paper, a pencil, and a ruler. It is also advisable to have a calculator, although the requisite computations are quite simple.

TYPES OF TECHNICAL ANALYSIS

With the thought that the market discounts everything, there is nothing more important for you to study than the action of that market. By saying that the market discounts everything I mean that future expectations and earnings are reflected in the price of the issue. Part of the value of a chart is that it tells you the direction of the trend and, by that, the direction of the next trade. Markets tend to move in trends; once in a trend, it is easier for the market to remain in that trend. The chart reveals the price action within an identifiable trend.

Price

There are several ways to view the price. Where did the trading price open? Where is it now? What was the high? What was the low? If it closed, what was the closing price? These data have many different time frames. For example, you might want to review a tick chart. A tick chart is a chart that plots each and every move that the subject of examination has made. Perhaps you prefer hourly charts, or daily, weekly, monthly, or maybe even yearly charts. These are parameters that you will define. Price is a view of the emotions of a stock; it shows elation and depression or just plain boredom.

Volume

The volume is also an important factor when studying a technical picture. Volume is usually represented by bars on the bottom of a chart; however, we do have equivolume charts, created by Richard Arms. These candles incorporate volume into the price. As the volume changes, the bar (candle) gets fatter with heavier volume and thinner with less volume; yes, it does muck up the chart. Volume has always been important as an affirmation of the current movement. Thus, if you see a stock climb on little volume, you just might be curious as to why nobody else finds this stock attractive; or is there perhaps a problem with the rally? In any case, the volume will either confirm or question the action seen. Later in this book, we examine how a lack of or a bulge in volume can provide an effective tool.

Time

Most conventional Western charting methods use time. In conventional charts found in newspapers and online, time is reflected on the horizontal line on the bottom of the chart and price is reflected on the vertical margin. These charts—candlestick charts, bar charts, and line charts, just to name three—always show the time frame being studied as it relates to the price of the security.

There are charting methods that totally disregard time, plotting only the movement. Point and figure charting is one very popular charting method where only the price counts. The up moves are Xs and the down moves are Os.

Charts such as kagi, renko, point and figure, and three-point break charts discard time. These methods concentrate on price alone. They are useful when used in combination with other charting methods. When using these price-only methods of charting, pattern and direction become abundantly clear.

Sentiment

So, how many bulls are lurking in the ring, looking to gore the bear? This is a sentiment indicator. Thus, we read polls, taken to ascertain how many investors, letter writers, and advisers are bullish; then, we compare those numbers with those of the bearish camp. We also use put/call ratios to help us understand the sentiment, as well as the VIX or VXN for that clue. Both the VIX and the VXN are volatility measures. They are calculated by using all quoted options, both puts and calls, in the two front months. The VIX is the "fear gauge" of the S&P 500 index puts and calls; the VXN is the NASDAQ-100 index puts and calls "fear gauge."

HOW TO CONSTRUCT A CHART

When a stock rallies there is usually a reason, both known and unknown, for that rally. What a technical analyst does, distinct from other
analysts, is to study the movement of a stock, sector, option, future index, or any product that trades at various numbers, with the objective
to understand where selling enters and where buying enters. Figure 1.1
shows an example of a point and figure chart. Note the Xs are the ups
and the Os are the downs. Notice how easy it is to see the direction that
the market is trading in.

The chart of a stock, commodity, bond, or any other instrument that is
being examined reflects possible inside information that has not been disclosed to the public; hope for the future, as expressed by investors; and
fear about the future, which would also be expressed by investors. Further demonstrated by the chart is supply and demand for the issue. Trends
can be seen and price patterns can be identified. This is only a small
amount of the information that can be deduced from a chart. Yes, it is true
that many technical analysts feel that the name of something doesn't matter; rather, what matters is the price. The earnings don't matter, and neither does much else about a company. What are of utmost importance are
the price, volume, and open interest in the subject.

While it is important to view a security on different time frames, a

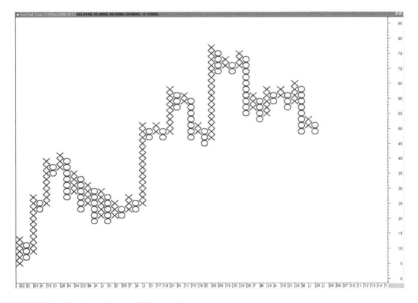

FIGURE 1.1   A point and figure chart.

longer point of view is a good starting point. It is like reading the background information before getting into specifics of the matter at hand. As an aside, I do feel that it is important to have all information available and I therefore always read as much as I can about a company, including the industry sector, the balance sheet, expectations, growth potential, book value, insider ownership, and, of course, earnings. It has been said, "The chart is a post-mortem and not a diagnosis; it is a result, rather than a cause, and its occurrence is afterward rather than beforehand." This handy quote is drawn from a meeting report in the *Journal of the American Statistical Association* (Volume 20, Issue 150, June 1925, p. 245). But there were others at that meeting, reported in the *Journal*, who explored the importance of plotting reactions. One speaker, Ray Vance, defended charting as being "such a measure of business happenings, and such a survey of the results which have followed these happenings in the past, as will permit the anticipation of security price movements with worth-while approximation to accuracy" (p. 247). Thus, we have a well-stated purpose for studying this discipline.

Devotees of this discipline expect to learn of future behavior from patterns of past behavior. What we say is that the leopard doesn't change his spots; he just moves them with him. Our purpose is to study those spots to learn where and how they will behave in the future. It is interesting to note that the quotes in the preceding paragraph are from the year 1925, not from a recent article. We use technical analysis to predict, with some degree of accuracy, the probable action to be seen in the very near future. We do not use crystal balls, bones, or any sort of extrasensory perception (ESP) in our studies; we use facts, numbers, and behaviors that were demonstrated in the past to help us interpret the probable pattern of behavior in the future. Isn't the market just a reflection of human behavior and can we not predict that behavior with some degree of certainty? Surely other disciplines do the same. Wouldn't you expect that a psychiatrist would outperform a CPA in his predictions of human behavior? Unless you believe that humans are not responsible for the moves of the markets, you will have to agree with this assessment.

Creating a Simple Bar Chart

We start off with the basics: how to construct a bar chart, shown in Figure 1.2. The bars we're to construct will be vertical bars. In the United States, markets have an open, a close, a high, and a low. All of these numbers are reflected in a single bar measuring the time interval under study. That time frame could be seconds, minutes, hours, days, weeks, months, years, or decades. The simple information needed for construction of that bar is found in Figure 1.3.

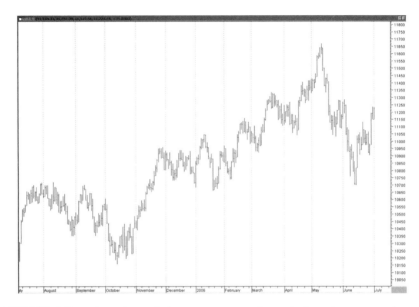

FIGURE 1.2 A bar chart of the Dow Jones Industrials (INDU). Time is shown along the horizontal axis and price is shown along the vertical axis.

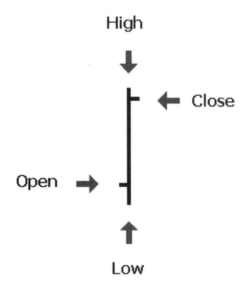

FIGURE 1.3 Single bar.

Figure 1.3 shows a single bar with arrows pointing to:

- The open of the designated time frame.
- The high.
- The low.
- The close of that time frame.

The bar's length from top to bottom is the length between the absolute high point and the absolute low point of that time frame. If it were a daily bar, it would be as long as the range of the day; in other words, the bar would reflect the movement from high to low, or low to high, in that time frame being plotted. That distance between the high and the low is called the range. (See Figure 1.4.)

Now we have a bar. On one side of the bar, a notch is indicated, where the price opened. In other words, if the stock had a range from a low of 11 to a high of 16, the bar would be 5 units long. If the open was at 13, a left notch would appear there. If the closing price was 15, a right notch would appear there. Now, you have drawn a bar representing one day's trading in that security. A time frame can be as short as a tick and as long as you wish to make it. We generally use intraday charts, those drawn on the activity of the security or futures contract during the trading session; daily charts, ones that represent one day of trading; weekly charts, which represent one week's activity in a single bar; and monthly charts, which represent the entire month's activity in a single bar. (As an aside, some plot only the closing price of the subject. Those charts are called line charts.) When we plot all of these daily numbers on graphing paper, we get a chart that can tell us volumes about the stock on which it is drawn. The chart would be a bar chart.

Example So, let's get started by drawing a single bar on a piece of graph paper. Let us say that the stock opened at 13.75, it had a high of

FIGURE 1.4 Bar showing the range of 15.75 to 12.75 with tick marks for open and close.

FIGURE 1.5   A single bar showing the range.

15.75 and a low of 12.75, and the close was 14.75. This information can be plotted on a single bar, which will be just as long as the range of that stock activity during the time of measurement. The range is the difference between the high and the dead low of the time frame. Here we see that the high was 15.75 and the low was 12.75; therefore, the range is 15.75 minus 12.75, or 3 points. (See Figure 1.5.)

Now, it would be nice to know where the stock opened; therefore, we'll nick that bar on the left side at 13.75. Then, we will nick the bar on the right side for the closing number of 14.75. As you can see, on a single bar we have plotted a lot of information that we can readily view. If we do this on a continual basis for each defined time frame, whether a day, a week, or even a minute, we will create what will look like a chart. This chart will tell us in pictures what has been the activity in the stock or any other tradable product.

Take your favorite product and measure it in this way. It could even be a mutual fund, a sector of the market, a futures contract, or an option. As an exercise, just plot it for a while and see what you come up with. This charting method uses time and prices as inputs. Perhaps you haven't noticed, but volume and open interest are not valid in constructing a bar chart. That information comes into play with other types of charting methods and also, by simple calculation, can be plotted on the bottom of your chart. This will be discussed in detail in Chapter 2.

TOOLS THE TRADER CAN USE

We have briefly mentioned the kinds of charts that you can review or draw, but what do I use? The chart types are many, and the studies that you can apply to these charts are even more numerous. For example, you can use stochastics, moving average convergence/divergence (MACD), Average Directional Index (ADX), or Bollinger bands. We use these studies to ascertain information as to overbought, versus oversold measurements, standard deviations from the mean, moving averages, and so on. There are probably hundreds of analytics that you can apply to a chart for guidance. You could virtually spend all day looking at these. The trick is to find studies that will help your analysis. Find the studies that work for you and stick to them rather than looking at new studies. If stochastic indicators are working for you, use them. Don't use MACD because your pal does, if it doesn't work in your trading or analysis. Be consistent in the studies you use so that you don't waste your time adding studies. Spend your time analyzing the market.

Inside the Pits

If you can visualize a group of about 150 or so men standing in a circle on a series of steps yelling at one another, you are beginning to see what I see on a daily basis. Not only are these guys yelling, jumping up and down, and flailing their arms, but they are also trading. This is how the open outcry market works. We stand on tiered steps with the reporters in the middle, at the podium, and in the four corners of the upper tier of steps. The reporters write down the trades as they occur, publishing them so that the public can see what is being traded. The reporters input the data into handheld PDAs, which transmit the information electronically; any corrections or additions are made by the caller, who is an employee of the exchange who oversees the reporters. The caller also ensures that the market is fluid and, when occasion arises, will post a "fast market condition." The caller, an exchange supervisor, can halt the trading and is in charge of opening and closing the market. The locals stand on the lower steps and the paper brokers on the upper steps. Paper brokers are the executing floor brokers who work for brokerage firms. This arrangement is designed so that the orders can be given to the paper brokers standing on the top tier of the ring. Around the trading ring there are booths with phones, order-receiving machines, and a bunch of clerks manning the phones. These are the guys who take the orders from the trading desks, time-stamp those orders, and hand them to the brokers to fill.

Many times you work really hard to get an order filled. You yell and scream and you still aren't filled even though a guy on the other side of the ring has the order you want. Ideally, you would love to run up to the guy and say "Buy it," but you can't. So you try to get his attention by screaming and jumping. Why can't we run up to the guy and say "Buy it"? Because we have rules for the floor community to abide by, and that would be charging. Just imagine that a broker has an order that half of the ring wants. They would run over and smother the guy! Thus, at the

(continues)

New York Board of Trade charging is illegal and a fineable offense. In other words, when a person is offering a contract and you wish to buy it, you have to make your wants known to that broker by yelling and jumping up and down or in some way catching his attention, but you may not run up to him and buy it. That is considered charging.

These rules are enforced by the Floor Committee. The Floor Committee is made up of traders who police their fellow traders. Now, it looks, feels, and sounds like total confusion. In my ring, to add to that confusion we had identical twin brokers. It was bad enough that you had to make sure the guy you traded with agreed that you traded with him, but now we had identical twins. In the heat of a fast moving market, good luck remembering who you were trading with! Then we have the clowns who, when the market gets slow, pull pranks on each other. Once a guy was walking around with a paper arrow on his back for hours, and several have sported tails hanging from their trading jackets. I have had a sign that said "Kick me" on my back.

Those who are new to the ring are spurred. What is a spur? Well, these paper spurs are taped to a guy's shoes and the entire ring starts to whoop and holler, much like in a rodeo. We even do a sort of square dance with the victim. I remember when they spurred me. I didn't realize it for at least 15 minutes. All I wanted to do was to trade and these clowns were whooping and hollering. I was looking up at the boards and not at my feet. Eventually, I found the spurs. One guy was so unconscious that he took the subway home with his spurs on. The entire floor gets into the act. People come over from other rings on the floor and look to see who got it this time. It really disrupts trading, but it is all done in good fun.

HOW I USE TECHNICAL ANALYSIS

I use technical analysis every day in my work in stock selection (for a possible buy, sell, hold, or short); allocating money into sectors; buying, selling, or shorting of indexes; purchasing or selling bonds; or any aspect of the market to be examined. For me, it has always been the ruler and the pencil in combination with the other studies. I do not need a computer to analyze an issue, just a chart of the issue. It's nice to have the add-ons to help with your analysis, but the basic pencil and ruler will help you decide if the issue is going up or going down. Although that does not seem hard to do, you wouldn't believe how many people get wrapped up in computer studies and fail to look at the direction of the chart! Many people use too many different indicators and simply confuse themselves. Then there are those who use so many oscillators and indicators that they spend their entire day trying to figure out the problem. That's not a good idea; sometimes the simple approach works best.

Patterns have always played a role in my observation of the markets. They give you clues—buy me, short me, sell me. The studies then confirm or deny that clue. I love using five-period exponential moving averages to keep me in, or get me out, on a short-term basis. I also use combinations of exponential moving averages to help define a trigger point. These are all discussed later in this book, so you too can assess the value of the combination of analytics, sentiment indicators, pattern recognition, and plain old line drawings to get a handle on the trade. After all, we are in to win, not to lose; therefore, any tool that works will be declared useful.

As a trader and a newsletter writer, I use many combinations of technical analysis and some that I have developed on my own to aid in giving me information that is useful to trade. Before I ever set my foot into the ring or place the electronic trade, I review my charts. I always start with a daily chart of the subject market. Yes, I then look at weekly and monthly charts. These give one a feel of the market, the lay of the land, so to speak. It is like reviewing a map before you take a trip. You plot your course, your stops, and whatever else you might need to review, before jumping into the car and driving off. I do the same sort of thing with stocks, bonds, indexes, futures, or whatever it is that I intend to trade. There have been many times that I have reviewed the charts and decided not to trade for a number of varying reasons. One leading reason is: risk/reward trade-off. Is the risk worth the reward? This is something that you will need to look at for every investment you make.

FUNDAMENTAL ANALYSIS VERSUS TECHNICAL ANALYSIS

First and foremost, it must be said that both fundamental and technical disciplines are worthy endeavors for student study. Fundamental analysis uses company information including balance sheets, assets, liabilities, inventories, taxes, debt, duration, convexity, book value, debt to equity, and so on. According to Robert D. Edwards and John Magee in *Technical Analysis of Stock Trends*, Sixth Edition (New York Institute of Finance, 1992, p. 4):

> *The stock market fundamentalist depends on statistics. He examines the auditors' reports, the profit-and-loss statements, the quarterly*

balance sheets, the dividend records and policies of the companies whose shares he has under observation. He analyzes sales data, managerial ability, plant capacity, the competition. He turns to bank and treasury reports, production indexes, price statistics and crop forecasts to gauge the state of business in general, and reads the daily news carefully to arrive at an estimate of future business conditions. Taking all these into account, he evaluates his stock; if it is selling currently below his appraisal, he regards it as a buy.

It should be further noted that dividend discount models and other modeling will be used by fundamental analysts in evaluating the issue in an effort to uncover the value of the issue. Naturally, with debt securities much of the same criteria are used as with stocks, along with measures of duration and convexity and the issuer's ability to pay the debt. In futures, weather, planting, supply, and demand are important inputs in fundamental analysis of the futures markets.

Both disciplines should be used in obtaining a knowledge base before an investment is to be made. The use of both techniques in concert will bring to the user a full symphony of information that can be applied in the search for superior returns. Technical analysis provides a pictorial historical representation of the subject of examination. It is rather like an electrocardiogram, which depicts heart activity, in that it shows a pictorial view of past actions. The analyst uses the knowledge of past actions to make projections of future actions. Just as a baseline electrocardiogram is useful to the physician for comparison with a current electrocardiogram, so, too, a past chart of a particular market action is valuable when comparing it to a current chart. The chart is an examining tool to evaluate price action of the subject under study. Ultimately, technical analysis is the study of human behavior. Should you believe that it is a spooky discipline, you would have to disregard any study of human nature and behavior as well, including that of Sigmund Freud.

Who but humans program the machines that will automatically buy or sell? Are money managers human and do they react to situations that could be emotionally charged? Of course they do. Is the individual investor emotionally charged when he/she reacts to a situation? All of these individuals move markets; markets don't move themselves, but, rather, they are driven by humans. Thus, technical analysis is in some ways a study of human behavior. It is a war zone and we have to learn how to react under stress and what past behavior under these circumstances has been. Technical analysis is very different from fundamental analysis in that the chart, or price action, includes all the fundamental information available, together with the information about the stock—information both public and nonpublic. You can see in a single chart the hysteria, depression, and elation felt by the market at a specified time. Why nonpublic? Because it is assumed that, should there be a leak of insider information, that leak will be made apparent in the action of the stock. The compliance-enforcement arm of the market views unusual activity and examines it, searching for possible insider information leaks. And the compliance enforcers also review the action in the options on stocks for insight into possible unlawful behavior.

A classical technical analyst wouldn't bother with the reading of earnings reports. Such effort is unnecessary in that it is reflected in the price of a stock, bond, option, or futures contract. It is presumptive that price action, volume, and open interest contain all requisite information (interest behavior, historically) and that information can be used to provide for the justifiable projection of possible future action based on previous behavior. There is nothing arcane or mysterious about this discipline. It can be learned through study.

When studying fundamental analysis, one learns modeling, economics, statistics, and so forth. For example, when studying the fundamentals of the subject (let's say a stock), the initial view is an overview of the economy, the industry in which that stock resides, and its relationship to the economic conditions. Should that initial overview yield a positive view toward the sector in which this stock resides, it will merit examination. To begin, the analyst will then review the company, its books, balance sheets, inventories, production, legal liability, and the like, all as part of an overview of that company. Then, the analyst applies modeling tools to evaluate the worth of the company.

All of these calculations and reviews are based on information provided by the company under examination. Now, that is an issue of concern to most skeptics. The information provided to the analyst regarding inventories, earnings, debt, leases, pension liabilities, health care costs, taxes, and so forth can be manipulated by the company being investigated, laying the analyst open to risk in that analysis, should such information be faulty. Who will ever forget Enron and WorldCom, glaring examples of companies providing false reports to the analyst community?

Technical analysis regards only the past price, volume, and open interest as important. While we will not disagree that dividends have an effect on a security, that effect is not nearly so great as to compromise the data under review. When studying technical analysis, one studies chart patterns, indicators, trend lines, and the like. The information gathered can be plotted. Anything that has movement can be charted; yes, even mutual funds. Any activity from which a measurement is created can be charted. Doesn't your physician chart your child's growth, telling you the percentile that child is in? It is possible for your pediatrician to plot your child's growth at age 2, and then to project the ultimate, adult height of that child. Is this ESP? No, it is calculable and probable, with a degree of certainty. You, too, may have had your various baseline statistics taken. Why, if there is no value to a chart? Clearly, it is important for the physician to see where our levels were before the onset of an incident. For example, if a cardiologist has a reference baseline electrocardiogram for you, the EKG can be compared with one created today, in an effort to see if there has been any change. Obviously, there is some change and, although this illustration relates to the medical arena, we can similarly apply our graphs and charts to the market's behavior, which is, peripherally, a reflection on human behavior.

We will be discussing line charts, bar charts, point and figure charts, renko charts, kagi charts, candlestick charts, and even market profile charting. All of these indicia have their own methods, but all lead to the same basis for conclusive evaluation. All methods of charting seem to illustrate three facts: that prices tend to move in trends, that history tends to repeat itself, and that the price of the subject of analysis has discounted everything known about the subject at that time. That is a lot to say in just a candle, X, or bar, don't you think?

We have heard many objections to our methodology; some critics even have the nerve to exclaim that when back-testing of the predictive value of the indicators or oscillators was executed on a computer model, the results proved that the system is flawed. Back-testing on a computer model will also prove, without a doubt, that fundamentals are flawed, as well. We are aware that the back-testing referred to was done on a computer model with default levels for studies; however, it is a failed method of discovery, because above all the machine cannot and will not replace the technical analyst. Many have tried to use computers to give rise to candle formations; they fail miserably. Thus, we will endeavor to pass on to you some of the little tricks that have been learned in the honing of this discipline. There is a basic human quality that is needed to interpret the data, a quality that computers cannot provide; even neural systems fail to be able to adjust and read visually that which the human eye can see, and the human touch can feel.

A further benefit of technical analysis is that it is universally understood by all technicians. Even with a visiting technician from Mars, speaking some unfamiliar language, the chart will tell a story, a story that will be understood. Yet another benefit of technical analysis is that it provides the ability to chart in whatever time frame is wanted. One can use hourly, daily, weekly, monthly, even tick charts to study a subject of interest. Many times, multiple time frames will be used to verify, illustrate, and/or confirm a belief. I use multiple time frames to confirm a trend. The signal is always stronger if all the time frames agree with each other. Yet, there is another tool of the technician, one that totally disregards both time and volume and studies only price action—that is, point and figure, renko, and kagi charting.

CONCLUSION

Charting is not a mystery, but rather an easy way of notating the movements in price of an issue. There are many ways to plot that information, and it can be broken down into many different time segments. In technical analysis, price is of ultimate importance. In some charting methods, time is also critical.

You really don't even need a computer to analyze a market that you are following; you do need the prices, volume, and perhaps the times of the trades. Technical analysis is to the market as an electrocardiogram is to a cardiologist, important information regarding the health of the subject. Markets are driven by people and as such are an extension of their emotions. As analysts we study the evidence and can increase the probability of a correct understanding of that emotional response by viewing the chart. That increase in probability enhances the bottom line, and isn't that what this is all about, anyway?

CHAPTER 2

Basic Charting

Technical analysis tools can give you an edge in your ability to make money. Before you learn how to use these tools for trading, you must first learn some of the basics. Like building a house, you have to start in the basement with the foundation. This chapter provides a frills-free summary of the following charts: line, bar, anchor, candlestick, market profile, point and figure, kagi, renko, three-line break, price and volume, and equivolume.

Of course no method is foolproof, but what you will learn here will give you a leg up on the competition by helping you minimize losses and enhance your rewards. As a trader, I can tell you that 90 percent of my trades are positive but I hold on to the losers too long and take profits too quickly. This is not an unusual characteristic, but one that should be corrected. When faced with doom and gloom, I am able to somehow reach into my bag of tricks and pull off a repair.

Those who regard mathematical statistics as uninformative will likely find the analytics derived from them as of trivial interest. I wish them luck in their further search for investment success. In the search for the means by which to comprehend the vagaries of the trading process, I know of no approach that is more rewarding.

CHARTS THAT CARE ABOUT TIME

To begin the study we will talk of charts that are time sensitive.

Line Charts

Charts allow you to visually represent data by plotting information on graph paper. In a line chart, time is plotted as the horizontal coordinate (the bottom of the paper); price is plotted as the vertical coordinate (either the right, left or both margins). When plotting a line chart, each closing price is represented by a dot that is then connected to the next price dot, yielding thereby an easy-to-read road map displaying the price of the subject under examination. (See Figure 2.1.) The date of the dot will be underneath it, referenced to the horizontal coordinate. The price will be referenced to the right or left margin, or perhaps, on both vertical margins.

For a daily chart, you plot one dot for the closing price; for a weekly chart (Figure 2.2), the Friday closing price will be the price dot on the graph; and for a monthly chart, the closing price for the month will be illustrated by the placement of that dot (Figure 2.3).

Many traders find intraday charts more valuable than the daily charts, because they allow you to build tick charts for any time frame desired. These charts will look different than the longer-term charts because they contain more data points than charts with longer time frames. The reason for this is that in very short-term charts you see more data and thus, in many instances, more noise. For example, I use

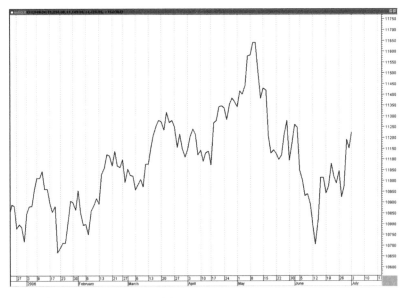

FIGURE 2.1   Daily line chart of the INDU.

FIGURE 2.2   Weekly line chart of the INDU.

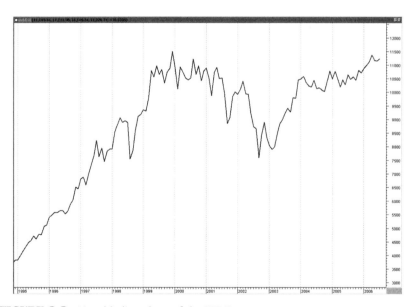

FIGURE 2.3   Monthly line chart of the INDU.

both 5-minute and 15-minute intraday charts when day trading. While longer-term charts are extremely important, and I do use them to get a better overview, they won't give me the intraday movement needed to make intraday trades. It is also valuable to see how the issue behaved during the day, especially if that issue had a significant move. Figures 2.4 through 2.7 are examples of short-term charts.

A tick chart (Figure 2.4) shows every movement that the issue has made; every burp and belch is recorded. As a result, you get a lot of what is called noise in the chart. I do not use tick charts in my everyday trading, but will refer to them when needed. A five-minute chart (Figure 2.5) plots a close, in the instance of a line chart, at the end of each five-minute period. Figure 2.6 shows chart plots the close at the end of each fifteen-minute period. Figure 2.7 plots the close at the end of each 60-minute period.

Frankly, as a trader I do not use line charts on anything but the very shortest-term charts, such as five-minute or tick charts. Even with a five-minute chart, my personal preference is for candlesticks because I find them far more descriptive.

Line charts are useful for demonstrating the movement and direction especially in longer-term charts like weekly charts and monthly charts. Sometimes with bar charts or candlestick charts the information becomes cluttered and the pure simplification of the line chart is an advantage.

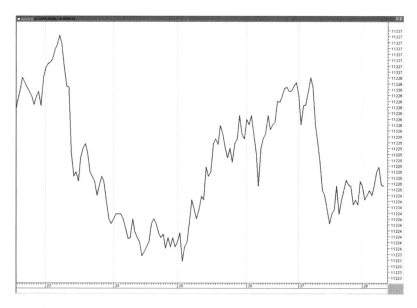

FIGURE 2.4   Tick chart (INDU).

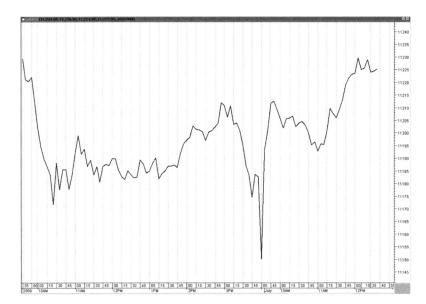

FIGURE 2.5 Five-minute chart (INDU).

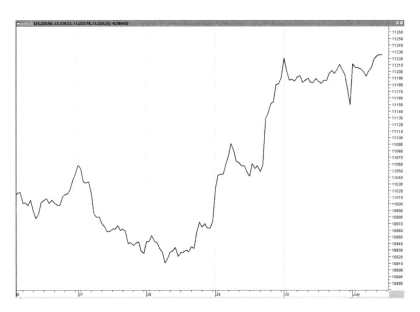

FIGURE 2.6 Fifteen-minute chart (INDU).

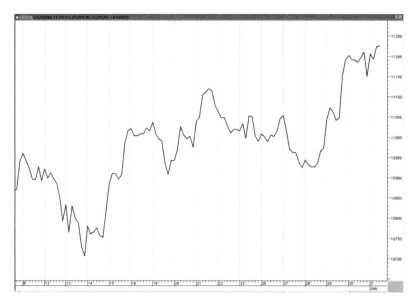

FIGURE 2.7   Sixty-minute chart (INDU).

Many times when I use a line chart it is to clearly show the trend of the market. Just the other day, I had to explain how I knew that gold was breaking out to the upside. It was far easier to just show the simple line chart to illustrate that point. Sometimes in trading, simple is better.

Bar Charts

As with line charts, bar charts give you a choice of time frames for this charting method. And again, the time or date reference will be plotted along the lower horizontal margin at the bottom of the paper (the x-axis) and the price will be plotted along the vertical margin of the graph paper (the y-axis). See Figure 2.8 for an example of a bar chart.

Bar charts can provide more information than can a line chart. The chart can show the opening price, closing price, the high, and the low of the period under examination. By looking at a single bar (Figure 2.9), one can determine both the range and the open and closing prices. None of this information is available from examination of a line chart, which shows only the closing price. The bar is drawn from the high to the low (or low to high—it doesn't matter) with a tick on the right indicating where the closing price would be found and a tick on the left where the opening price was. Thus, you immediately have a lot of visual information in a single bar.

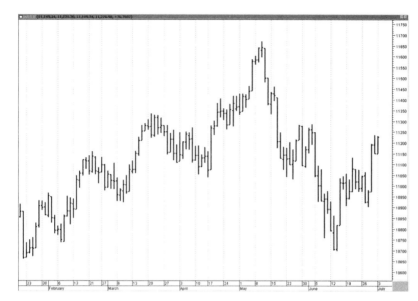

FIGURE 2.8 Bar chart (INDU).

FIGURE 2.9 A single bar of a bar chart.

Notice that the charts are arithmetic. This means that all the boxes or changes are equally weighted values. Now, this differs from charts plotted on a logarithmic scale; the reason is that log scales are descriptive of percentage moves rather than absolute moves. The purpose of using log scales is to make comparisons easier by way of visualization of a percentage move. This is especially important when comparing, for example, a $10 stock to one that is, say, $60, or an index that has a value of 50,000 compared to one that has a value of 320,000. A one-point move has a greater percentage value in the lower-priced study than in the higher-priced study. That is the purpose of log charts.

Anchor Charts

Anchor charts, the precursor to candlestick charts, are still an interesting charting method and, although I have never seen a charting package offering this unique type of chart, I feel that there is good value to this historic charting method. It may seem a bit naive, but the anchor chart points the arrow in the direction of the move. Thus, if the closing price was higher than the opening price, the arrow placed on the line is point up. Conversely, if the opening price is higher than the closing price, the arrow points to the downside. It is not very complicated, but is very useful visually. Steve Nison in his book *Beyond Candlesticks* (John Wiley & Sons, 2004) dates this method of charting to the "Kyoho Era (from 1716)." These anchors are created by drawing a single vertical line from the high end of the range to the low end of the range. The opening price of the range is depicted by a small horizontal bar crossing the vertical bar. The high is noted with what looks like an arrow, pointing upward if the close was higher than the open or downward if the open was higher than the close. When these are drawn they do look like anchors, as shown in Figure 2.10. I like these anchors because one can see the arrow clearly.

Candlestick Charts

The candlestick chart is the natural conclusion of a descriptive chart effort that began with the anchor chart. By that I mean that it seems as though the bar and anchor charts have limitations that are removed by the candlestick chart. Both the bar chart and the anchor chart begin with a vertical bar from the top of the range to the bottom of the range. Both the bar chart and the anchor chart mark the opening and closing prices. But the candlestick, besides showing the range from top to bottom and the opening and closing prices, offers some slight improvement to the visual information available: Between the opening price and the closing price, a body is drawn. We are not talking human, of course! This area is either

FIGURE 2.10 Anchor chart.

red/black or green/white. The body can also be described as empty or filled; white naturally is empty and black is filled. That area is described as the real body of the candlestick and, in fact, is the real body of the trading period under examination. If the open of the period's trading is higher than the close of the period, the candle will be filled (red/black). If the close is higher than the open, the candle will be empty. The real body shows only the distance between the opening price and the closing price and whether the open was higher than the close. Figure 2.11 shows an empty candlestick chart; Figure 2.12 shows a filled candlestick.

Now, for a trader that is a lot of important information to have available in a chart. The tails that are on the top of the real body and on the bottom of the real body represent the high print and the low print (the range). This, too, is valuable information for the trader to visualize. For me, it is far easier to see a black or red candlestick than to have to ferret out the tick marks on a bar chart. Why? Because it is far easier to see a black or red candle and know immediately that the closing price of that period of time was below the opening price. Many times, this sort of information can help you decide to buy or sell. Many traders become concerned if the price

FIGURE 2.11 Empty candlestick.

FIGURE 2.12 Filled candlestick.

closes below the opening price and view this as something that must be looked into.

Look at candles as a description of a war: the bears versus the bulls. If a market closes lower than it opened, the bulls gave ground to the bears and were unable to defend their position. It is a sort of failure, for the moment anyway. When you see a bunch of black or red candles, you know the bulls are on the run and that the bears have come out of hibernation and are on the prowl. Then there are patterns in candlesticks that will encourage you to be perhaps more bearish or bullish. This is a personal preference.

A very large-bodied candlestick is called a "long day." A small-bodied candlestick is called a "short day." A "long day" candlestick would flash to me that the market is moving violently one way or the other, whereas a "short day" would be almost quiet. A spinning top depicts trading that moved both higher and lower than the body of that candle. Figure 2.13 shows both an empty spinning top and a filled spinning top.

There are many rules regarding candlestick reading. There are formations and clues given by the groupings of the candlesticks and information that one can find about the chart being studied. So let's get some of these candles under control, right here and now!

Doji Candlesticks Let us start with a doji candlestick. A doji candlestick represents a market with a high, a low, and the unique marker of an open and a closing that are at the very same price. (See Figure 2.14.) To those who view this candle, which looks like a cross, it is an indication

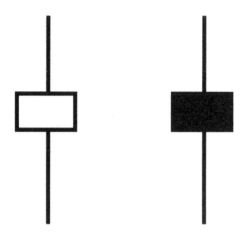

FIGURE 2.13 An empty spinning top and a filled spinning top.

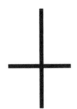

FIGURE 2.14 Doji candlestick.

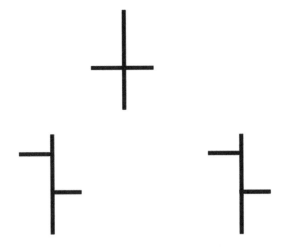

FIGURE 2.15 Another doji. A plain doji at the top or bottom of a chart is called a doji star.

that the market is in transition or just might be getting ready to change directions.

If you are in an uptrend and a doji candle appears, you might begin to worry that perhaps you are seeing a top in the market. (See Figure 2.15.)

A doji star is a type of doji candle that stands apart from the previous and following candle. Typically there is a gap up, then a doji, followed by a gap down. The dogi looks like a star on the chart; thus it is called a doji star.

If a doji candlestick has only one tail, this tells us immediately that the closing price was the same as the high or the low of the session. There are special names for these candlesticks:

- A *gravestone doji* candle has a long upper shadow and no lower shadow because the market closed on the low. This is a total failure for the bulls; the bears won the war and took the trade to the low of the day, where it closed the session. (See Figure 2.16.)

• A *dragonfly doji* illustrates that the bears lost and the bulls were able to carry the trade to the top of the range, where it closed. (See Figure 2.17.)

In Japanese candlestick charting it is the combination of various candles that is important and not a single candlestick (although there are times when a single candle can lead you to focus on the chart more carefully).

The interrelationship of the candles is important for analysis. Just one candle won't cut it. You must take the overview and analyze how one candle relates to another candle. I make up stories like the war already discussed in the description of the candlestick. For me it is a war; for you it could be a football game or a tennis game. The vehicle of the story is unimportant. What is important is understanding the psychological behavior of the trader, which is demonstrated in the candlestick and its relationship to the other candlesticks.

Market Profile

Market profile is a charting technique usually seen in the futures markets, rather than in the equity and bond markets. This is not because it is ap-

FIGURE 2.16 Doji gravestone.

FIGURE 2.17 Doji dragonfly.

plicable only to futures, but because it was developed by a futures trader. Here is some background information. Market profile was developed by J. Peter Steidlmayer (www.steidlmayer.com), who, as a trader at the Chicago Board of Trade (CBOT) in the agricultural pits, developed a method of following prices to help him in his trading. In the futures open outcry markets, trading is broken into various time sectors in the futures arena. Each bracket is a half hour long, punctuated by a bell or buzzer for the floor community. The opening and closing periods are handled separately. There is good reason for this, even though it sounds as if you were back in high school, moving on the bell from class to class.

This is important bookkeeping, forcing the brokers/traders to turn in their trading cards. These cards must be turned in to the appropriate boxes, located all over, within 15 minutes of the bracket's closing bell/buzzer, with all the trades that were completed in the previous bracket. These trades are then manually entered into a system that matches the trades with the opposing broker; this way, if there is a problem, that problem is found within a half hour of the execution or nonexecution of the trade and any disputes in price or size can be resolved quickly. I use the electronic version of a trading pad or card called the automatic trading card (ATC), which is a small personal digital assistant (PDA) on which I enter my trades, which are automatically matched. Further, if there is a dispute about a price, I don't have to leave the ring to correct the trade and can input the information while standing in the ring. Another advantage is that I do not need to employ a trade checker because I input the data myself. If I make an error, I can fix it without having to find a trade input personnel (TIPs) machine, which is where trades are input manually.

Each bracket is assigned a letter; the opening bracket will be "a," the next bracket will be "b," and so on. All the prices that trade in a certain bracket are noted on graph paper with the bracket's identifying letter. Thus, if you trade from 117.00 to 119.00 in the a bracket, you will place an "a" in each square from 117.00 to 119.00. Say in the next bracket ("b") you trade from 118.00 to 121.00; those trades will be placed on the paper next to the a's but will be noted as b; then the market trades from 120.00 to 118.50 in bracket c. In bracket d the market trades between 118.50 and 120.00. This is what an intraday chart using market profile might look like:

121.00 b
120.50 b
120.00 bcd
119.50 bcd
119.00 abcd

118.50 abcd

118.00 ab

117.50 a

117.00 a

Although the same method of charting can be used for any variety of time frames you desire, thus giving you a longer-range view of prices, it is interesting that once these charts are drawn, they look like a bell curve on its side.

As noted, the price runs on the vertical margin against time on the horizontal margin. So, what are we looking for with this method? Well, for one thing, we are looking for price equilibrium. This can easily be spotted; it's the place where most of the trades have occurred. In the example, it is between 118.50 and 119. The single prints at 117 and 121 are considered to be areas of instability where the market doesn't want to be. Obviously, that is important information for the trader. Recently we saw the single prints hanging above the U.S. Dollar Index and we then knew that should the U.S. Dollar Index enter that price it would quickly move away from this area of instability. This also allows the trader to see the next level up where comfort and equilibrium can again be found. As with a bell curve (a normal distribution curve), the center represents the area populated by the most trades or a place where both buyer and seller were comfortable with the trade. One major difference between the way a normal bell curve is drawn and this curve is that the market profile normal distribution is on its side. In other words, the x-axis is not the value or price line. The price line is moved to the y-axis. As in statistics, this center area represents about 68 percent of the trades that occur. As we move to the tails we get to the areas where only 5 percent of the trades occur and then to the areas representing only 1 percent of the trades that occurred. As with any normal distribution curve, the bell curve can be skewed, but our interest is not in its shape but rather in what information we are getting from that normal distribution curve.

CHARTS THAT DON'T CARE ABOUT TIME AND DATES

There are charting techniques that totally ignore time. The only thing that is important in these charts is the price. The dates of the trade are absent from the chart. Formations and trends are more easily seen in these techniques.

Point and Figure

Point and figure charting takes time and throws it out the window. Only price is important in this charting method. The method of denotation uses Xs and Os in the boxes on the graph paper at the appropriate prices. Initially numbers were used in the boxes to denote the trade; then they morphed to Xs, and today it is Xs and Os, although there is no hard-and-fast rule on that. What is important is that price is the only important thing and the only subject of the chart. Thus, if an equity or any other security, bond, future, or index remained stagnant and didn't change price, you would have only one X. You must decide what the X represents. Is it one point or two points, or 50 cents or a dime? *You* decide the moves you are going to chart. With low-priced stocks, fractions are generally used; with higher-priced stocks, single points are used. The parameters are shown in Table 2.1.

In the case of Google, you moved from the initial one point per box to two points per box, and now it is four points per box! Google began trading at 85, then rose above 100, and recently traded as high as 465. Thus, you have adjusted your boxes as per the price of the security. You are moving the values as you would on logarithmic graph paper.

For example, say you are trying to build a chart for IBM. Today, that security trades at about 80+ per share, so you probably would opt to use single-point notations. Thus, as the stock moved from 80 to 81 you would write down an X. Say the next move was to 82; you would indicate another X. The prices are indicated on the vertical margin. There is no time axis, just price. You continue marking your chart with Xs going upward in price until a down move of one point is seen; then, you move your pencil to the next column and write an O at the appropriate level. This indicates that you are no longer going higher but have had a reduction in price. Many traders say that to change your column you need a three-box move; thus, if you use that method, you need to wait until three points have been removed from the stock price before you can proceed to the next column. We will come back to this method later in this chapter, but for now that is an adequate description.

TABLE 2.1 Box Size for Charting Price

Price of Security	Points per Box
0–5	$1/4$-point move per box
5–20	$1/2$-point move per box
20–100	1-point move per box
100–200	2-point move per box
200+	4-point move per box

CSI Meets the Cotton Exchange

It was back at the old trading floor, on the 8th floor at #4 World Trade Center, that the following incident occurred. At that time, the New York Futures Exchange (NYFE) occupied a ring adjacent to that of the Cotton Exchange. (The Cotton ring may be familiar from its use as a trading floor in the Eddie Murphy movie *Trading Places*.) At that time, the New York Composite index was actively traded and sported good open interest and volume.

Open interest can be defined as those contracts opened and not yet closed. For example, if you were short a contract, you would eventually have to buy the contract to flatten your position or deliver the product; that would count as one contract open interest. If you were long a contract that, too, would count as open interest. Basically, open interests are positions that will have to be flattened by expiration, unless delivery is anticipated. Today, there are 63,000 contracts of open interest in March coffee. Before that contract expires, that open interest will fall to zero, indicating that all longs and shorts have exited the market and nothing remains, unless delivery is wanted. Those contracts wishing to have the product delivered will remain open. The customers are notified that delivery is pending in plenty of time to flatten the unwanted positions. It is interesting to pay attention to open interest because it represents liquidity in the contract. For example, the Russell 1000 traded at the New York Board of Trade has open interest of 91,000 contracts for the March contract.

Jack (all names have been changed in this story to protect the not-so-innocent) is an excellent day trader who used to trade the New York Composite index in the futures arena. He uses point and figure charting to solve the mystery of the direction of the market and is known to walk around with a huge roll of graph paper marked with Xs and Os in his jacket pocket that he tapes together to continue his charts. Every time the market moves a prescribed distance, Jack marks the graph with an X for going up or an O for going down. Jack was known as a "Pig" because of this habit of snagging all trades. We also called him "dirt-nickeler." Why? Because he would better your bid by a nickel or be cheaper by a nickel just to snag the trade.

Tim's trading style can be likened to a parasite: He tends to nag you for the same quote on the same strike price 15 times without ever trading, because he is looking for a number that may have some astrological value to him (and more on *that* later in the book). In any case, it is an annoyance to those having to give him the quote time after time. Both traders are locals, which means they trade their own money and do not fill customer orders.

(continues)

One fateful day, Tim wanted the contracts and Jack, as was his habit, stepped in front of the trade to take it for himself. You must understand that because of the placement of the stars in the sky, Tim had to buy the contract at that exact moment in time. As it happened, I (still a newbie to floor trading) was standing between Jack and Tim and had to hustle myself out of the way, not wanting to get in the middle of the mess. There was a huge argument about the trade, Tim screaming at Jack and demanding the contracts. Spittle flew, they were eye to eye, and the altercation was the result. As it turned out, Tim stabbed Jack with a pen quite by accident and drew blood.

When the dust cleared, both were banned from the floor for the day and were levied fines for misconduct. Another trader decided to block off the area with yellow tape, like a crime scene. He then took a piece of chalk and drew a picture of a pig on the steps in the ring, curly tail and all, with a sign: "This is where the Pig fell"!

Pig fight in the ring.

Three-Box Reversal   A three-box move in the opposite direction of the previous trade is required before a move to the next column can be made. We noted previously in Table 2.1 the size of the boxes according to the price of the security. As an example, if a stock is trading at 17.50, you need only need a half-point move to enter an X or an O. Say the market has been rising and the stock is now at 17.75; no mark is made. Why? Because the fraction needs to be at least 18 to be posted in the X column.

Following this train of thought, the market has been rallying and now the stock is selling at 19.50; you quickly take out your pencil and place an X on top of the previous X at the place marked 19.50. The following day the trend continues and the stock goes to 20; you mark another box in that X column. The rally continues and now the stock closes at 20.50, terrific, but no mark in the X column. Why? Remember stocks from 5 to 20 require only a 50-cent move to get a posting, but stocks above 20 require a whole point move. You put nothing in the box and wait.

Just to answer the question before it arises, if the stock moves from 19.25 to 19.75 it is a 50-cent move, but only the 19.50 will be recognized. The fraction above that level will be ignored.

Now our stock is at 30 and the rally stops. We have a rather large column of Xs. The stock trades at 29, but we do nothing, because we need a move of three boxes to make a notation in the opposite direction. We must wait until the stock trades at or below 27 to move over one column and start our Os. We fill in the 29, 28, and 27 with Os. That is the three-box reversal. See Figures 2.18 and 2.19.

It works on the upside as well. Now our stock is trading at 21; the next trade is at 22, then 23, and finally 24, when we can move over a column and place our Xs in the boxes at 22, 23, and 24. That is all there is to that.

Kagi

Kagi, a Japanese charting system, is similar to point and figure charting with regard to noting the changes of price. However, one of the big differences is that instead of Xs a single line is drawn continuing the direction of the previous trade until that price is violated by a predetermined amount, whereupon a new kagi line is drawn in the next column in the opposite direction. (See Figure 2.20.) As Steve Nison stated in *Beyond Candlesticks*, "When prices penetrate a prior low or high, the thickness of the kagi lines changes."

As you can see, this charting method allows the analyst a pictorial view, saying "Look here!!"

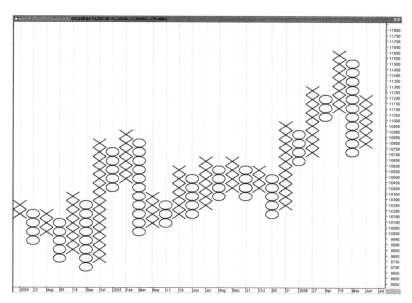

FIGURE 2.18   Point and figure chart of the INDU with one-box reversal.

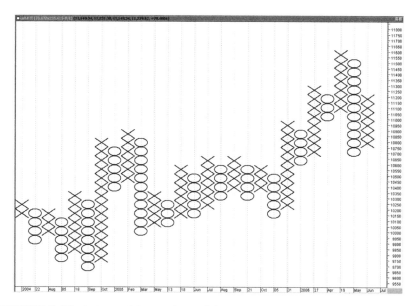

FIGURE 2.19   Point and figure chart of the INDU with three-box reversal.

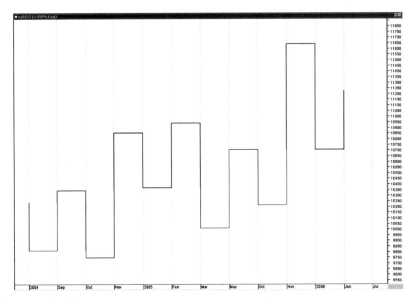

FIGURE 2.20   Kagi chart.

Renko

In renko charts, each line of the chart is called a "brick." (See Figure 2.21.) If the market is rising you will have all white bricks, but as the market retreats these bricks are black. Some software uses red and green instead of black and white. The price axis continues to be the vertical margins, or the y-axis. The price is noted on the vertical margin of the chart. The bricks are all the same size (an assigned value); the only deviation is the last brick of the previous direction which is a partial brick, at the top it is called a "neck" and at the bottom it is called a "black shoe." Thus, you have a chart that has some similarities to a point and figure chart yet is distinctly different. You will get a sell or buy signal visually when the brick has a neck or a black shoe. The beauty of this type of charting is that rallies and retreats really stand out as events, and it is easier to discern various patterns along with failed rally or failed sell-off attempts.

Three Line Break

The three-line break is similar to renko charting except that to paint a new line next to the previous line, the new price must have broken or exceeded the previous three lines' low or high (Figure 2.22). This means that if there is no change in the market, there is no line. In *Beyond Candlesticks* Steve Nison says: "To determine if the market has started down, the

FIGURE 2.21 Renko chart (INDU).

FIGURE 2.22 Three-line break. (Copyright © 2006 eSignal. Published by eSignal, www.esignal.com.)

low price of the last three rising lines must be broken on the downside during the fall. On the other hand, to determine if a decline has ended, the highest price of the last three declining lines must be exceeded on the upside" (p. 268).

Volume Charts

It is customary when looking at charts to view the current volume at the bottom of the chart, such as in Figure 2.23. The volume seen can be for any time frame desired. Futures provide volume but a day late, and certainly volume is not available on intraday open outcry markets. What is open outcry? It is the ring where traders buy and sell the futures contracts as opposed to the electronic platforms available today. Electronic platforms do provide current volume and volume for any time frame desired. There are some charts that plot volume and price on only one chart. The price continues on the vertical margins but the volume is noted on the horizontal margin. It is interesting to view these charts because they illustrate clearly the price of the heaviest volume. These charts can be for any time frame desired.

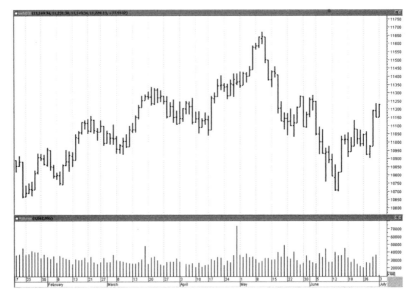

FIGURE 2.23 Price and volume chart (INDU).

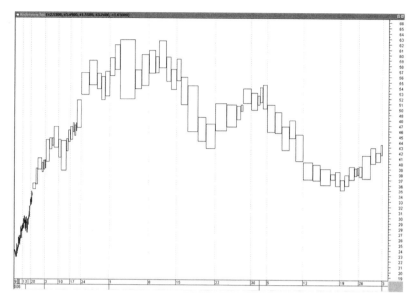

FIGURE 2.24 Equivolume chart (Andersons Inc.)

Equivolume Chart

As advertised by the title, these charts—an offshoot of candlesticks—describe the volume of the trade with the width of the candlestick. (See Figure 2.24.) If the rally in the candles was on high volume, the candlestick will be fat, depending on the volume, of course. If the rally is on low volume, the candlestick will be thin. That is all there is to this topic.

I don't like equivolume charts because they clutter up my field and hamper my ability to draw lines and figure things out. I would much prefer using price and volume charts in another window.

CONCLUSION

There you have it, the basics of charting. You now have learned how to chart using line, bar, anchor, candlestick, market profile, point and figure, kagi, renko, three-line break, price and volume, and equivolume charts. It is up to you to decide which charting format works for you. All of these charts have one thing in common: They visually show you the direction of the market and help you mark out the resistance and support levels.

There is no right or wrong way; you must decide for yourself what you feel comfortable using. Market profile is frequently used by day traders in commodities but is almost unheard-of in the equity arena, probably because this charting technique had its beginnings in the commodity markets. I prefer candlestick charts in my work and in trading. I find absolute value in line charts for demonstration because they are so clear. Point and figure charts are valuable in identifying trends. I use market profile along with the candlesticks and find them very helpful in my trading.

CHAPTER 3

Identifying Trends and Calculating Support and Resistance

Before we can discuss support and resistance lines, it is essential to decide the trend of the market. Obviously, it is important to first stand back from your market and review the direction of the prices. These prices can either go up as in an uptrending market or go down as in a downtrending market. The trend therefore can be defined as the general direction of a market. An uptrend can be seen as a market making higher highs and higher lows, whereas a downtrending market will be seen as a market making lower highs and lower lows. Sounds simple, right? In fact, it is very simple to see—so long as you don't have a trade on!

While some traders use a method called scalping for day trading and appear to just buy and sell all day long, making a little bit of money on each trade without the intention of investing, many find it important to discover the direction that the market is going. Why? Because if you see that the market is in rally mode, you will be less inclined to be short that market. You would then consider buying the dips as a strategy. The trend is the big picture, the direction in which the market is going. Every trend has its peaks and valleys, these are points within a trend where the market rests after a move, but when looking at the big picture, one should stand back and look at whatever kind of chart one is using and then decide if the action is to the upside or the downside. Here is where point and figure charts and line charts (introduced in the previous chapter) actually make the determination of direction very clear. While there are intermediate trends in between, the emphasis should be: Keep it simple, stocktrader (KISS).

After reading this chapter, you should be able to tell if and when the market is trending, as well as what direction (up or down) it is trending.

43

The next step is identifying the nature of the trend—secular, primary, intermediate, short-term, or intraday. All of those descriptors (discussed later in this chapter) indicate the length of the trend.

Your first job is to discover the direction of the market (the trend) and then to identify the duration (length of that trend). After this is done, you can then look for areas of support, where the market participants view the market as cheap, and resistance areas, values considered to be expensive. Only then can you apply that information.

OVERVIEW OF TRENDS

There is an old and wise Wall Street saying: The trend is your friend. This isn't a bad way to look at the market and in many instances it is correct. Most futures traders are contrarian traders. A contrarian trader trades against the trend and will take a contrary opinion of the market. This is rather like playing with a loaded gun, and in truth many times it feels that way. Say the market opens up five points higher; such a trader will short the market in the belief that the rally, for now, is done and the trader wants to capture the retreat in the market. He sells the contracts out and waits for the market to fill the gap left on the opening. Most times he will be right, but of course there are those times when he is really wrong and the adage is right. Ouch! The adage supports the belief that if the move appears to be in an upward trend, invest in it and don't fight the direction of the market. I have many black-and-blue marks from trying to fight the market. The adage encourages you to ride with the tide instead of fighting the current.

Then there are just those plain old bears lurking around. Before we continue, permit me to clarify one point: Futures traders are generally trading from the short side of the trade. That is, they are short. Why? Because the downside velocity is usually must faster and more forceful than is the move to the upside. Markets tend to take longer to rally than they take to retreat. The trader is looking for the quick fix; thus he tends to that side of the trade.

In the ring at the New York Board of Trade we had two such stalwarts—bears out of hibernation and prowling in the ring. These guys didn't care about the trend and were just die-hard bears. I had no choice but to name them the "Bear Brothers." These two would short the market all morning and then buy back their shorts in the afternoon. I don't believe they ever took a bullish position. What was really scary was that in the old days there was a designated room on the floor where traders could light up and smoke their cigarettes. Their corner room looked down onto Liberty Street and the firehouse. After a visit, the smell of smoke would linger in your hair and clothes for days and everyone knew where you had been. You felt and smelled like a dirty ashtray. The walls, originally white, were now a deep yellow from the smoke. The vertical shades were also yellowed with the residue of the smoke. Yet the room was never empty; it always had traders going over their trades while puffing on their butts. Both our Bear Brothers were inveterate smokers and could usually be found in that room. The frightening part of the act was that they would leave the trading ring to go for a smoke, usually with trades on. That is, their positions would be open and they would just go out for a smoke.

Perhaps it doesn't sound too serious until you realize how large such a contract actually is. Permit me to tell you: The contract is huge! Today, the contract is trading at $700, which is the base. Multiply that base by $500 per point and you get the value of this contract (this is one contract—not two, not three, just *one*). The value of this contract is $350,000; for each point change, the value of the contract appreciates or depreciates $500. (The minimum tick on a trade is .05, which is $25; therefore one point is $500 or $25 times 20.)

Both Bear Brothers were not small players by any measure; they'd think nothing of shorting between 10 and 50 contracts at a clip. Ten times $350,000 is over three and a half million dollars' worth of risk. That comes down to $5,000 per point. Being short 10 contracts was nothing for these guys; they would do that just for giggles. And yet they would abandon their positions for a nicotine fix. I remember seeing one of them looking over his pink copies of his trading cards. The trading cards or pad on which the trades are written have three copies, a white copy which goes to the exchange and then a pink copy and a yellow copy. These were pages and pages of trades and he was sitting there, trying to figure out how many contracts he was short. He had no clue, just a gut feeling. His attitude could be summed up by the following statement: "Screw it, I'll just short more." Why? Because the market refused to go down. This guy was unclear on "the trend is your friend"—he must have been out for a smoke during that session. He didn't lose every day, though. Many days he emerged a huge winner; otherwise he would be doing something else now (in his former career he was an attorney—go figure). In the late 1990s and early 2000s mega-rally, the market volatility was enormous. There were sell-offs that were large and rapid, allowing people like him to make a lot of money. We had many days when the market went limit down, only to reverse and close up on the day. Then there was his day trading, at which he certainly was a pro. He would nickel-and-dime his way into profits (scalping), day after day after day. I remember him sitting in the smoking room during the Long Term Capital Management debacle and, after realizing that he was long rather than short, running back to the ring to reestablish the short.

Beyond the Ring

Many traders have interests beyond the trading ring. We may jump around like maniacs, but we are real people, too, and we come from diverse backgrounds. One trader is a pharmacist (no, he doesn't deal on the floor), and there are more than a few attorneys and even a couple of medical doctors. People flock into this business from all walks of life.

I used to spend hours with one trader checking out different recipes. He specialized in the hottest peppers, all grown at his home garden on Long Island. He kept me in good supply of Jamaican hots, Scotch bonnets, and many other really hot peppers. He would eat the stuff straight, with nothing to cool it. Then he discovered that if he added butter and a cracker, voilà: a good afternoon treat. From that experiment, I learned to chop up the hot peppers and mix them into margarines or soft butters for use on vegetables.

While in our "backup center," a temporary residence for the floor after the World Trade Center trading floor was destroyed, another trader used to send her clerk to Flushing in Queens to pick up Chinese food—which she ordered in Chinese. Then she would divvy it up among those of us who opted in on the deal. Once, she ordered special gourmet cheese and fresh bread baguettes to enjoy with the cheese. Some of the traders who didn't like the smell of all those cheeses got pretty annoyed.

Food is not just a hobby on the floor; it's an obsession. As you have probably gathered by this time, the floor is loaded with type A personalities. Most of us don't sit still well and we tend to drive nontraders crazy because we multitask constantly. We have been called hyper but we really are not. My children always warn people, "Don't let Mom drink any coffee!" It seems that we have boundless energy, which we need to direct somewhere and trading is the target. Much like a glutton, as a trader you really can't get enough of a good thing and will gorge yourself with a good trade. Part of this behavior is similar to our food obsessions. While many of us will not overeat only because we will get fat, we will overtrade and overextend our accounts. There has to be something in this, right?

There are those traders that will always go against the market, but they have a plan to day trade taking advantage of the mini price swings in the market. What is not visible to the observer is that many of these traders are aware of the direction of the market and are trying to take advantage of the rallies and retreats in a normal trading market. It is much like the ebbing and flowing of the tides. They go out and they come back in, and within each rising or receding tide are individual waves. The trader's job is to ride a wave and paddle back out for another ride.

What Is a Trend?

A trend tells you in which direction the market is going. Are the highs getting higher and the lows getting higher? If the answer is yes, it is probably an uptrend. Are the highs getting lower and the lows getting lower? It is probably a downtrend.

These basic trends appear in all charts. You, no doubt, have heard of trend-following programs. They capitalize on the trend by discovering the trend and adding to positions as the trends go forward. In an effort to discover the trend, the use of longer-term line charts is of great value. It will be fairly easy from viewing the chart (weekly or monthly) to see the direction in which the market is moving. That direction would qualify as a primary trend. Primary trends last from nine months to perhaps two years. Other trends are intermediate trends (one to nine months) or short-term trends (two to four weeks). Electronic trading has added another category: intraday trends. These traders focus on only the day, rather than a longer-term prospective.

This is all well and good, but the market moves up and down; so how do I know where I am? Easy. If the highs are getting higher and the lows are getting higher, you are in an uptrend. As mentioned before, if the highs are getting lower and the lows are getting lower, you are in a downtrend. Each trend has a squiggle in it. We find ourselves going up, pausing, and then perhaps resuming the up move. These pauses can be called consolidation periods. They are marked by lighter volume than is seen on the up move. Sometimes it even looks as though the trend could be changing direction, but it doesn't. These are stair-step patterns, common in market moves. (See Figure 3.1.)

Within these movements we find levels at which some selling becomes apparent, probably due to some profit taking. These levels, which the market interprets as levels at which the price seems a bit high, are resistance levels. Here's a quick analogy. You own a store, and you place an item in the store and it sells. You figure that it is too cheap; otherwise it wouldn't have sold so quickly. So you raise the price. The item continues to sell out and there is a demand for more. You again raise the price, but now the item is taking longer to sell. You are beginning to see some resistance to the price. If you assign a price that is even higher, the item may completely stop selling. That is a pretty good description of resistance. Then if you reduce the price enough, the buyers will return for the product. This is an example of price support.

Now let's translate that into the price of a security. Support is a level

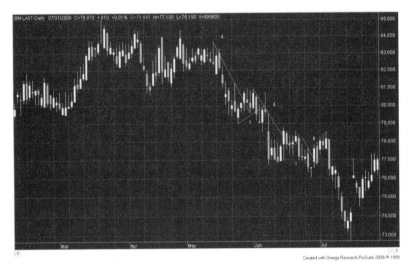

FIGURE 3.1 Stair-step chart showing a rally and stopping and another rally and stopping again. (© TradeStation Technologies 1999. All rights reserved.)

at which the buyers appear and start to purchase the asset because it appears reasonably priced or a bargain. Resistance is the level at which the sellers feel that the price is higher than it should be and begin to sell the product, preventing the price from rising further or causing resistance to the rise in price.

Classifying Trends by Duration

Many of you have heard analysts speak of different trends as though they were strange, mysterious events that only analysts are smart enough to know. To put an end to this, I am offering you simple, brief descriptions of some of the mystery terms defining duration or the length of time of the trend:

- A *secular trend* lasts from 10 to 25 years. A long time? Yes, but these trends do last that long.
- A *primary trend* lasts a year or more with a 20 percent move associated with it. It may last for several years. We are currently in the fourth year of a bull trend that is a primary trend. You might encounter several primary trends within a secular trend.
- An *intermediate trend* persists from weeks to months. Clearly, you might find several intermediate trends within a primary trend, within

a secular trend. Obviously, these trends are in the opposite direction to the primary trend. Thus you can have an intermediate bear trend within a primary bull market. It is called a correction.

- A *short-term trend* lasts from days to weeks.
- An *intraday trend* is the trend that is established in some period of time less than a day. For example, I use 15-minute charts, 30-minute charts, and 60-minute charts when looking at intraday trends. Each time frame may have its own uniqueness about the trend. The 15-minute chart could look like an uptrend but the 30-minute chart might not show that trend.

As a trader who doesn't keep positions for a long period of time unless they are associated with an option position, the short-term and intraday trends are the primary trends I use for trading. The advent of electronic trading technology has spurred a developmental interest in intraday trends and trading. For intraday trading I use a 5-minute chart and use a 15-minute chart for confirmation. Before I trade that market, I will look at the longer-term trend of the market by viewing the daily, weekly, and monthly charts.

Directions in Trends

There are three directions in a trend: the initial move, the consolidation of that initial move, and the continuation or reversal of that move. If one has an up move, one would expect the market to rest at some point. Such a rest is called a consolidation or a period of backing and filling. Why backing and filling? Because that is precisely what the market is doing; it is going back and forth within a narrow range, gaining enough energy to continue its journey. Consider this: A rally takes a certain amount of energy (whether buying or selling) and once this energy has been consumed, a rest is needed to review that progress and to reenergize. In a bull trend, one will frequently observe a market rally persisting for a few days (usually less than seven successive days) and then resting. When the buying dries up, that rest is seen. People sit and wait to rethink the run-up; as mentioned, that period is usually identified as consolidation or backing and filling. Both terms describe a market trading in a narrow range.

In a sideways market (see Figure 3.2), the pullbacks are shallow and the advances of the consolidation are equally narrow, producing a sideways pattern on the chart. As traders, we know that this pattern will resolve to either one side or the other. We also know that the longer a pattern persists, the bigger the move will be when that move begins (an uptrend in Figure 3.2). The same can be said of downtrending markets (Figure 3.3). These markets dive and then rest, consolidate and resume

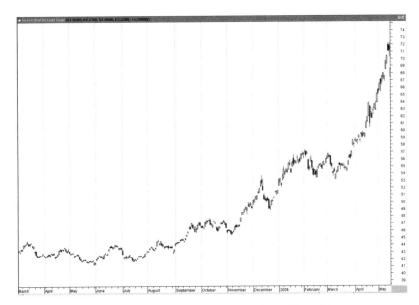

FIGURE 3.2   Trending charts going sideways and up, like gold or copper.

FIGURE 3.3   Trending charts going down, like coffee. (Copyright © 2006 eSignal. Published by eSignal, www.esignal.com.)

their retreat. Again, one has three possible moves. Perhaps the third leg will be a reversal; that too, is certainly possible.

Consolidations look like congestion on the chart. The areas of consolidation are generally seen after a large move in one direction. The length of time of that consolidation will vary and no information obtains that can be anticipated. Consolidations are sideways moves with narrow definable ranges. We might compare this range-bound move to consuming a huge meal, followed by a rest period to digest dinner before considering dessert. Markets behave similarly, bingeing and resting. This is a period of equilibrium or consolidation, a period when the market is like a creature taking a nap or going nowhere fast. Markets often seem to be either black or white. Periods of consolidation are periods that assume a hue of gray. These periods of consolidation can take the form of rectangles, pennants, flags, and the like. These are periods of accumulation or, in the case of downtrends, distribution. The longer these periods last, the greater the resulting moves.

For an uptrend to continue, each high gives way to a higher high, and each pullback is a higher pullback than the previous pullbacks. If you cannot observe this action, it's probably not an uptrend. Further, as each attempt at a new high is achieved it is higher than the previous high. On the pullbacks, each dip is higher than the previous dip. Clearly the reverse is true for a downtrend. Each rally is met with selling and that level of selling begins at a lower point. Each pullback creates a new low for the move.

Volume

More than average volume during a trending market—whether up or down—underscores the value of the move. For an uptrend, ideally you'd like to see increasing volume on the upside with light volume on consolidations. It is thought that volume usually leads price; therefore, if you see volume picking up and the market advancing it would not be unlikely that a move to the upside will develop.

The opposite is true for the downside. If you see increasing volume on retreats, with thin volume on advances, it is likely that the trend will be to the downside.

Time

The more time spent in consolidation, congestion, digestion, or range-bound trading areas, the bigger the resulting releases will be. Visualize a spring that is being compressed; the longer the pressure builds within that spring, the higher (or lower) it is going to go. The newer the resistance or support level is, the more reaction you will see as the market challenges that new level. The information you gain by watching the reaction to new support or resistance levels will tell you a lot about the future of that trend. For example, the first time the Dow Jones Industrial Average penetrated the 11,000 mark, a retreat was seen the very next day. The retreat was large enough to tell us that to stay above this level was going to be a problem. There was a decline in the Dow of 250 points.

More recently, the Dow again moved above the 11,000 level, but this time the rally continued for two days before a retreat was seen. That retreat was smaller, telling us that perhaps the rally had more to go on the upside. Of course, that spring retreat led to a summer rally with the Dow making new highs. Although the Dow is often referred to as "the market," it is not the market; it simply is an average of 30 stocks with varying weights, which tends to skew the average. Although the Dow made new highs, the S&P 500, a broader measure of companies, may not have made a new high. Recently the Dow made a new high with only 30 percent of the stocks within that average making new highs.

Trading Tips

If you see a trend, you have to realize that others, too, are seeing the same thing. If you see resistance, others see it as well, play with that knowledge, and sell before you get there. Remember to put in stop-loss orders when you play that game, just in case you are wrong and have read the chart wrong. The market seems to have numerous orders at round numbers. If you don't put your orders there you will have less competition for the trade. If you can discover what the upper edge of the trade is, based on history, put your limit orders in early. Remember the electronic platform logs your order on a first come, first served basis; you only stand behind market orders. Market orders always take precedence over limit orders. A market order means fill it *now* at the next best price. If the offer is there, lift it for the buy; or if the bid is there, hit it for the sell.

Life in the Ring

In the trading ring, we naturally stand next to our friends or people we like, or we stand in a very desirable spot like next to the option side of the ring. That spot has been known to feed many tidbits to hungry traders waiting for a mispriced trade. In the ring, the contracts frequently are given to the selling or buying broker's friends. They may not have been the first in line but are rewarded with these tasty morsels. When trading on an electronic platform, this favoritism is removed. For me it is

(continues)

preferable, but for others the old way is the better way. Much of the trading in the ring is like watching the ocean's waves crash on the shore and then retreat. Audible volume becomes louder as the trading in a particular pit picks up. You can't hear that in electronic trading. Watching the ring to see who is buying or selling is another important piece of information that is missing on the electronic platform.

For example, in coffee many of us are aware of which brokers are executing the roasters' orders and which brokers are executing the funds' paper. We can make a judgment about the trade from that information. If the locals are long, we know that they will want to be out of their positions by the end of the session. Most locals buy and sell contracts all day and go home flat. Flat means that they own nothing and are ready to start the process over again the next day. During the day, as you stand in the ring you can tell if the locals are buyers or sellers. This information is valuable for the end of the trading day because you know which side of the fence they are sitting on and what action they will have to take to flatten their positions. This sort of information is not available on the electronic platform.

The trading ring can be a confusing place. We stand on tiers in a circle facing the other traders. With about 100 to 150 traders in an active ring it is difficult to get things done. I have become accustomed to checking my trades as I do them. When I began trading in the ring I would check the trade twice just to make sure the person I traded with knew or accepted the trade. This annoyed the other traders, so I have learned to check the trades quickly and then check the system to make sure the other guy agreed with my trade. Most of the time it is easy to make eye contact and simply signal that you either bought or sold the contract with the other broker. In coffee, however, we are blessed with identical twins. In a busy market it is difficult to figure out which twin you traded with, and believe me, they enjoy that chaos.

On occasion, we have visits in the ring from the back-office personnel to remind us that we might have a position that is beyond our risk manager's comfort zone. I remember many times when John Harris would come to the floor. Usually, his appearance meant that somebody was in trouble. He was known to take the badge right off the jacket of the trader! He would appear looking for margin money. In futures, margin is due immediately or you will be liquidated. Bern, who worked for Spear, Leeds & Kellogg, would come over to the ring and stand next to the offender. She would cozy up to the offender, and sure enough the position would be reduced to a more comfortable level. If Bern's supervisor, Sharon, showed up, you knew you had a *big* problem. These types of things on the floor are accomplished quietly.

OVERVIEW OF SUPPORT AND RESISTANCE

Support is the level at which a stock, index, bond, or commodity becomes cheap enough to encourage buying. It is the level from which buying commences. If you own XYZ stock and that stock suffers a decline, the point at which that decline stops could be called a level of support. Will it last? Time will tell, but what you can see is that, for now, the reduction in the price interests buyers and they support the issue at that level.

Resistance is the price point at which sellers emerge because they believe that the price being offered is higher than it should be. If the price were fair, they would keep the issue. Another area of resistance is seen after an issue has suffered a loss and returns to a previous level. Just think about it: Investors bought the stock at 30, and it is now 15. They likely are saying to themselves: "Where can I get out without losing too much money?" Usually, at about this time, they start praying and promising to never again buy these shares! Then the shares come in with great earnings and the price returns to the 30 area. The shareholders now think to themselves, "Wow, I finally am even on the trade. Let me out of here before it tanks again." This behavior is akin to selling a contract to satisfy the "pit god" so that the market will rally. Yes, these things really happen.

Resistance as Supply

Resistance is not necessarily a new high. It can be an area of supply where previous longs (those who own the shares) get out of their position. Supply refers to the area on a chart that indicates that a lot of people bought their stock there; thus, there is a lot of supply of stock available. This is the area where resistance is found to a further advance.

Support as Buying

Support can be seen as an issue retreats from a higher level and finds buyers interested in the issue. It is a point at which the issue is deemed a good value and one that should be purchased. It would be a good place to cover a short position. A short can be defined as selling that which you do not own; you must replace the issue you sold.

Say you thought the stock of IBM was high at 83, which was its resistance area, and you decided to short the stock at 83. The stock declined to 76, where it stopped declining and seemed to find buyers at that level. You might purchase the stock at 76 to cover the short, pocketing the 7 points you earned via the decline of the stock. In futures, you don't have to borrow the issue; you can simply short it without permission. You will have to purchase the futures to close the position.

Support levels are important areas to define because should the support level fail to hold the issue up, you might have a greater sell-off than you expected. Further, should that support level fall, that level typically will become the new resistance level for the issue.

Identifying Consolidations and Resistance on Charts

There are many ways we see consolidations on a chart. It could be a rectangular continuation pattern, an accumulation pattern, or even a trading range. Consolidations are areas that are narrowly bounded and the price seems to stay there for a while. The longer a consolidation lasts, the greater the move usually will be when this pattern ends. That is not to say that it will be up or down, but it will likely be a very large move.

Resistance is an identifiable point on the chart, and often previous resistance will become future support. Suppose you purchase a stock at 30 and it move to 40, where it has a tough time getting through that level; 40 is the resistance. This is the point where this stock has met selling pressure strong enough to prevent a rally from taking this issue further. One day, though, you notice that the stock is trading at 44. You look back and see that eventually that stock met with enough buying pressure to push it higher. The stock may again pull back to the former resistance area of 40, but this area now becomes support for the stock.

Let's go even further. We witnessed the stock moving above the former resistance level and trending higher. This stock had been going sideways for a time and this move represents an upward trend in this issue. Moves like this are common in the markets. It seems as though the markets move in fits and starts, in a somewhat jerky fashion. In an upward-trending market stocks go up and rest, then resume the up move. Or the trend could be in the opposite direction, causing a downward-trending market.

Volume

If there is heavy volume at the support/resistance area of a move, it is an important area. That makes sense, when you think about it. The more volume the market has to get through, the harder the move will be. If you have to run through piles of beach sand, you get tired and it is difficult for you to do that for an extended period of time. It's the same with the market if every tick is met with sellers; the progress to the upside is going to take a while until all the sellers are removed. Another problem is that as the supply of stock is removed, more may appear. Then the price may be reduced to help the sale. Let us put it in terms of a product on the shelf at the store. If that product is priced on the high end but is desirable, it will sell. However, the purchaser will resist the price if it is perceived to be *too* high; the product will remain on the shelf as resistance. The more products on the shelf remaining unsold, the harder it will be to raise prices. Should the product become more desirable, the public will pay a higher price for it and then that supply will disappear, allowing the merchant to raise prices again.

The same rules apply to stocks, commodities, bonds, options, or any market for that matter. As the product becomes more desirable, greater quantities will be sold, even at higher prices. Volume usually leads the price, as is demonstrated by this example.

Time

Time and volume play a very important role in evaluating the value of the support and resistance areas. The longer the issue remains at the price, either support or resistance, the more important that level will become. It is perceived as a level that is cheap enough to attract buying, or expensive enough to attract selling. The longer a price range remains in effect, the more important that range will be. It is also noteworthy that if the range or resistance and support levels have been recently formed, they will cause more of a reaction than the longer-term resistance and support levels. Of course, the most recent resistance and support levels are the most important data.

Breaks in Support/Resistance

Most novice chartists mistakenly believe that support and resistance numbers are hard-and-fast numbers, which, of course, they are not. They have a bit of elasticity to them. It is usually an easy fix to make an adjustment for this elasticity. Simply use numbers that are valid only if they are elected on a closing basis. You may ask: "Well, how do I know if the numbers are good numbers?" The answer is that you don't. What you *do* know is that these numbers are guidelines for you to use as a reference point. Let me tell you why these numbers could fail to help your analysis on an intraday basis. Often, stop orders are placed at a previous high or a previous low, at the point of resistance/support. This is not a secret; it is a common occurrence, especially in the futures market. Let me bring you into the world of a trader. He is trading in the ring and we are nearing a resistance level. The rest of the traders are watching the same number and are calculating where the stop orders could be resting. As we approach the number, it almost appears that they try to force the trade toward that number, just to elect those stops. Once the stops are elected, the market will break the resistance/support lines and probe that area. That is why those numbers don't hold on an intraday basis.

Recall earlier in this chapter that the Dow Jones Industrial Average was halted at the 11,000 level for a while. Eventually, this number was overcome and you immediately saw the averages trade higher and then settle back below that number. What you witnessed was a probing of resistance, which discovered resting stop orders, which were then elected. Once these orders were elected, the market settled back below the resistance level. On occasion, it takes two days of probing those resistance/support levels before the market returns to the former level.

Should the resistance/support numbers fail to contain the market, you will immediately notice a rally/sell-off. Probes are small moves, whereas breakdowns and breakouts are moves with teeth in them. Always remember that if you see the resistance/support lines, you can believe that others see them as well.

CONCLUSION

As we have shown, a trend can be identified by higher highs and higher lows in an uptrend, and lower highs and lower lows in a downtrend. Trends are easily identified by looking at the daily, weekly, and monthly chart formations. A word of caution, though: It is possible to derive different trend information conclusions from examination of these various charts. For example, the daily chart might be showing you an uptrend, supported, too, by the weekly chart, whereas the monthly chart might show a different picture.

Support and resistance levels are important for the chartist to solve for an exit or entrance strategy. These points, where the market perceives the price to be excessively expensive or excessively cheap, are easily found and should act in concert with one another. Support is the level at which the price of the issue entices buyers to nibble and buy. Resistance is the point where the price seems to have a lot of trouble getting higher. When it seems as though it takes an inordinate amount of volume to push the issue up, you are viewing resistance, much like a brick wall can be viewed as resistance. Many times the market senses the resistance area and simply jumps over that level, only to retreat within two days. This information is important for you to have so that you enter and exit the markets at the time best suited to your goals. Sometimes, we will buy or sell at any price. There may be other reasons for this behavior but most of us like to enter or exit the market when we believe it is at a level that usually sees buying appear or a level that will resist further advances.

CHAPTER 4

Pattern Recognition

I have learned the hard way what works and what doesn't. While it is nice to know all of your choices when it comes to tools of the trade, the trader has only one real interest—making money. For this purpose, this chapter highlights my favorite patterns, the ones that work for me.

FANS

Fans are not a regular pattern choice for my intraday usage, but they *are* applicable for daily, weekly, and monthly charts. This is because a fan (a triad of trend lines) can be drawn for either an uptrending or a downtrending market. A requirement for the drawing of a fan is that you must be able to identify a correction; a point at which the trend seems to be stalling, possibly reversing course, must be shown. Three fan lines are drawn from the beginning of a correction—one, in fact, that may show multiple retracements. The first fan line is drawn starting at the low point of a trough or the high point of a peak. It is preferable to have three points to connect. In an uptrend this first line will trace higher lows; in a downtrend, lower highs. These points are reaction points. See Figure 4.1 for an example of this line drawn in the NASDAQ-100. The primary fan line is a simple uptrend or downtrend line.

The main reason fans are valuable is that they indicate to you when to bail out of a trade. Thus they are especially helpful for those of you who are loath to relinquish unprofitable trades.

FIGURE 4.1   Example of a single fan line. (Copyright © 2006 eSignal. Published by eSignal, www.esignal.com.)

Let us now look at an example of a fan in the S&P 100 options trading on the Chicago Board Options Exchange (CBOE). As the market backs and fills after an ascent or descent, the first fan line can be drawn from the peak of the rally or the trough of the decline (Figure 4.2). From that level, a reaction will be seen where the market will back and fill. The second line is drawn to what is viewed as resistance/support (Figure 4.3). The market continues lower or higher and another level of resistance/support is found, where the last fan line will be drawn (Figure 4.4).

So what is the big deal about fan lines? Well, you can find the level at which you will place a stop with the use of fan lines. For example, if you own XYZ stock and it rallies and runs up 25 percent in a handful of trading days, you, of course, are happy. Then the market reacts to this rally with some profit taking and the market retreats (Figure 4.5). You are now getting nervous. Then, the market rallies again, only to retreat another time (Figure 4.6). A third rally and retreat then create the third fan line (Figure 4.7), a line that should be the place where your interest in said stock ends. Fan lines can be used on the downside as easily as they can be used on the upside and are helpful tools for viewing the validity of the move. They also provide a stop point for you, the trader—a place where you cover your short or sell your long.

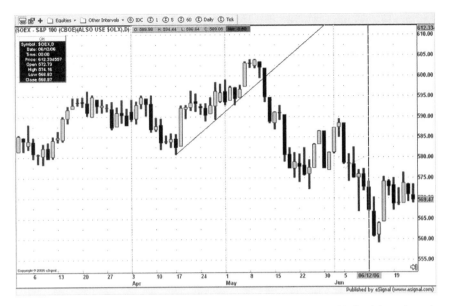

FIGURE 4.2 Fan line one. (Copyright © 2006 eSignal. Published by eSignal, www.esignal.com.)

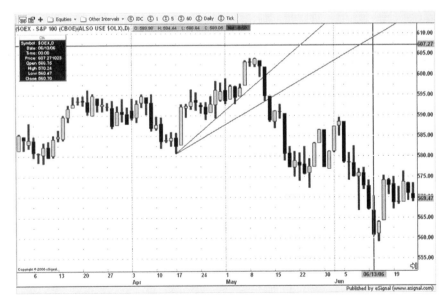

FIGURE 4.3 Fan line two. (Copyright © 2006 eSignal. Published by eSignal, www.esignal.com.)

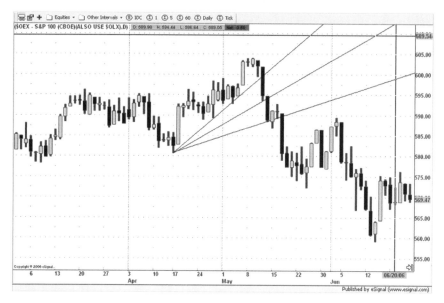

FIGURE 4.4   Fan line three. (Copyright © 2006 eSignal. Published by eSignal, www.esignal.com.)

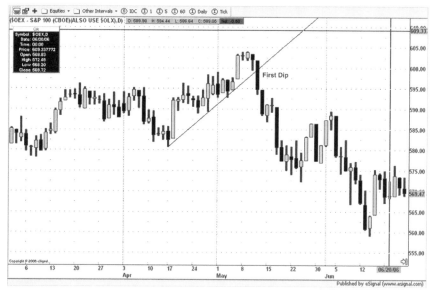

FIGURE 4.5   Fan line one, first dip. (Copyright © 2006 eSignal. Published by eSignal, www.esignal.com.)

FIGURE 4.6 Fan line two, second dip. (Copyright © 2006 eSignal. Published by eSignal, www.esignal.com.)

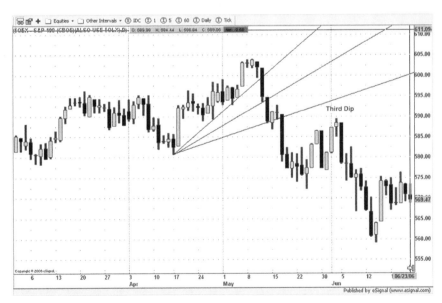

FIGURE 4.7 Fan line three, third dip. (Copyright © 2006 eSignal. Published by eSignal, www.esignal.com.)

These sorts of fan lines are especially good for the person who isn't ready to give up on the stock. Here you are allowing the stock plenty of room to prove you wrong. The first time the stock fails and rallies, you have hope; the second time you think this might be it, and by the third shot, it is either make it or get out of the trade. You are giving the issue three chances to prove itself. This works on the short side as well, of course, using downtrend fan lines.

FIBONACCI RETRACEMENTS

Leonardo Fibonacci was the Italian mathematician who studied a sequence of numbers where each number is the sum of the two before it. Zero plus 1 is 1, 1 plus 1 is 2, 1 plus 2 is 3, 2 plus 3 is 5, 3 plus 5 is 8, and so on. There is a strange thing about these numbers: Take a Fibonacci number and divide it by the number before it in the series and you will get: $1/1 = 1$, $2/1 = 2$, $3/2 = 1.5$, $5/3 = 1.666$, $8/5 = 1.6$, $13/8 = 1.625$, $21/13 = 1.61538$, and so on, with the results approaching what is often called the golden ratio, given a Greek letter Phi (Φ). (This, of course, is a very watered-down version of the math.) This numeral is thought of as the divine proportion, a recurring number in science, postulated as the answer to everything. The number we are speaking of is 1.618 or its inverse, which is 0.618, known as phi (ϕ).

He also found that these numbers occur frequently in nature. For example, most flowers have petals that are number 3, 5, 8, 13, 21, 34, 55, 89, and so on, all of which are Fibonacci numbers. If you were to dissect a shell's spirals you would find Fibonacci numbers again (and you'd be well on your way to understanding the mystery of Dan Brown's *Da Vinci Code*). There is also a cute study on the reproduction of rabbits that highlights the Fibonacci numbers. There are games you can play with pine cones, vegetables, fruits, leaves, and so forth, all Fibonacci spirals and all fun to find.

I'm sure you want to know how this relates to a chart. Whether it's a self-fulfilling prophecy or just a fact, you will find these numbers in the chart patterns of stocks, bonds, and commodities. Key numbers to remember are 38.2 percent, 50 percent, and 61.8 percent—these are called Fibonacci retracement numbers.

Say the market moves from 10 to 20; it would be expected that once the market pulls back, the support will be seen at 10 minus 38.2 percent or 6.18, further at 10 minus 50 percent or 5, and 10 minus 61.8 percent or 3.82, where 10 represents the recent gain from 10 to 20; thus, the first support number will be 20 minus 3.82 or 16.18; further support will be at 15, which is 20 minus 5; and the final level will be at 20 minus 6.18, or 13.82. That is the typical application for Fibonacci retracement numbers by traders. In a strong market, we expect to see only a shallow 32 percent retracement. Fifty percent retracements are quite common and are not viewed as unusual, whereas 68 percent retracements are more serious and would indicate that the market is not very strong. We can go further and include Fibonacci arcs (discussed in the next section), time zones, and fans.

One trader, TJ, uses these numbers for support and resistance on a short-term basis. Actually, Fibs—as we call them—are used by many traders and seem to work well. Our first job as technicians or traders is to find the beginning of a move and to identify it. The move could be to the downside or to the upside. For the downside, it is the point at which the market ceases to decline. You now have identified point number 1. The next job is to identify the point at which the rally fails or the trend seems to end; that is point number 2. Once we have these two numbers, we know the distance between the top and the bottom, or the range of that move. Now, we apply the Fibonacci retracement numbers of 38.2, 50, and 61.8 percent to the range of the move to discover the points at which the market will find support. (See Figure 4.8.)

FIGURE 4.8 Chart of a range from the top of the measurement to the bottom of the measurement. (Copyright © 2006 eSignal. Published by eSignal, www .esignal.com.)

The same method works on the upside as on the downside. We discover the range and then apply the Fibonacci number to find support and resistance levels. As a trader on the floor, I simplify it even further, taking the range under examination and dividing that number in half and also into thirds. From the bottom number, I add the one-third retracement number. Voilà! A resistance number is found.

Inside the Pit

As a local working on the floor of the New York Board of Trade, I've met hundreds of people. The floor population is nominally about 1,500, including clerks, trade input personnel (TIPs), and runners. Trading in the ring brings you closer to those with whom you trade, sometimes too close. When we're not trading, we usually pass the time by doing crossword puzzles and Sudoku, and playing games like liar's poker. We used to have a poker game (you know, with a felt cloth, chips, and cards), but the officials soon put an end to that.

One very prominent local has a daily bet with those who would like to bet on the market closing at unchanged. For a mere dollar, you can bet on this with the payoff being usually around $500 and a dinner at the Peter Luger Steakhouse either wet (with liquor) or dry. Many of us do take that bet. Actually the trader would like nothing better than for the market to close at unchanged. This guy sells options and of course wants the market to remain where it is, so offers the bet as sort of a donation to the "pit god" to keep the market in line.

TJ bases his bets on the market on astrology. He has plotted every minute of the day with the objective to tell you just when the market is going to rally and when it is going to fall. In fact, much of his work depends on traders' astrological markers. He has fastidiously made a record of each trader's date, time, and place of birth. (Note to those who may want to try this at home: These things can read quite differently depending on time zones, so he uses Greenwich mean time.) For example, Lou has an inclination to be bearish on the financials. (Bearish is an understatement. He says he will never own a stock with a price-earnings (P/E) ratio of greater than 1. I call Lou Perma-bear because he is permanently bearish.) TJ has Lou's birth date and hour of birth. He calculates and plots Lou's chart, then interprets this chart and the chart of the market to decide whether the market will have a good or a bad day. If Lou's chart is good for the day, the market should retreat, if Lou's chart is bad, well, a rally is coming.

In any case, TJ is a constant user of the CQG charting program. But why use charts if the stars know it all? I certainly can't answer that, but I do know that he is a dedicated devotee of Fibonacci retracements.

TJ and his many tools.

Further, I add one-half the range to the bottom number and, there it is: another resistance level. The final two-thirds number is added to find the next level of resistance. Generally, I find that should that number fail to keep a lid on the market, it is a reversal and not a retracement. The same method can be employed to find a support number, but in this case, we subtract the one-third from the top to find the first support level and then one-half for the second level and two thirds for the last level. It is clear that a shallow retracement or support level will include only a one-third retracement, a more substantial one will be one where 50 percent is given back, and the weakest of all will be the two-third number.

FIBONACCI ARCS

Fibonacci arcs (Figure 4.9) are drawn with a compass using the absolute top and absolute bottom of the stock—not just the range of a move (by range I mean from trough to peak or vice versa within a larger picture). A compass draws the arcs at 38.2, 50, and 61.8 percent, noting where there will be support and resistance on the price of a security or whatever is

FIGURE 4.9 Fibonacci arcs. (Copyright © 2006 eSignal. Published by eSignal, www.esignal.com.)

being charted. For a better description of this, John Murphy in his book *Technical Analysis of the Futures Markets* (Prentice-Hall, 1986, page 410) says: "Fibonacci arcs incorporate the element of time. By using a retracement measurement similar to the fan lines, three arcs are drawn from a top or bottom based on 38%, 50%, and 62% Fibonacci parameters. These arcs identify time as well as the place where support or resistance is likely to function. Fan lines and arcs are usually used together."

FIBONACCI FANS

These lines are drawn at a 38.2-degree angle, a 50-degree angle, and a 61.8-degree angle from the topmost or bottommost point on the left side of the chart. They can be drawn from the top of the peak or the bottom of the trough and are used to show you the areas of possible support and resistance during downward and upward corrections.

CHANNEL LINES

After you draw your trend line, a second trend line can be drawn parallel to the original either above or below it. For example, if the market is in

FIGURE 4.10   Channel lines. (Copyright © 2006 eSignal. Published by eSignal, www.esignal.com.)

rally mode, you have identified that the market is going up and will draw a trend line under the troughs of the rally. Identify the peaks of that same rally and draw a line along the peaks. You have now identified the continued expected range of the market. The same can be done with a downtrend, but of course in this case you are first drawing lines along the peaks. Drawing a parallel line along the troughs is easy, and it allows you to identify the expected range on the downside, as shown in Figure 4.10. Channel lines are frequently used by floor traders to discover the possible range and take advantage of it. The trader at home can easily do exactly the same thing.

REVERSAL DAY

Reversal days usually appear after an aggressive move, either up or down. Typically, the subject under investigation will make a new high or a new low and simply faint from the height or depth of the move. As Figure 4.11 shows (see May 12), you then see a large range for the day with a new high or new low printed and then a run to the opposite side of the trade. Notice the large trend developing and leading to a new high/low on the move. The

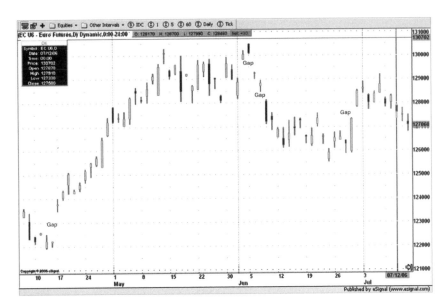

FIGURE 4.11 Reversal day. (Copyright © 2006 eSignal. Published by eSignal, www.esignal.com.)

next day there is a higher high or higher low, and then a print taking out the previous day's low or high.

For the bullish side, a new high is printed. The next day another new high is printed, but the previous day's low is also exceeded. This leaves a very large candle (or bar) on the chart. Sometimes these bars or candles are called outside days.

GAPS

There are two diverging thoughts on gaps. The first thought is that all gaps will eventually be filled, and the second thought is that they may *not* be filled. Frankly, it has been my experience that most gaps are filled. A gap is formed when the stock or whatever opens either above or below the previous day's high or low, respectively, leaving a hole in the chart where nothing was traded. On the upside, gaps are considered to be a sign of strength; on the downside, gaps are considered to be a sign of weakness. Figures 4.11 and 4.12 give examples of gaps.

Breakaway gaps represent the completion of a previous sideways price pattern and signify the onset of a significant move. See Figure 4.13 for an example; this is the first gap seen on the chart. Breakaway gaps are considered

FIGURE 4.12 Gaps. (Copyright © 2006 eSignal. Published by eSignal, www
.esignal.com.)

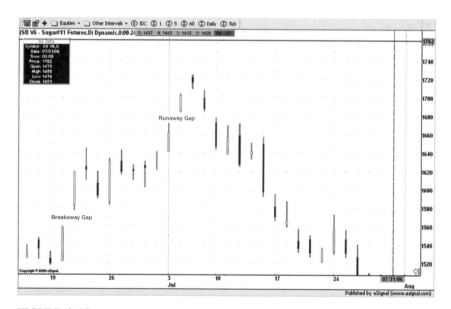

FIGURE 4.13 Breakaway and runaway gaps. (Copyright © 2006 eSignal. Published
by eSignal, www.esignal.com.)

to be bullish or bearish inasmuch as they signify the end of a previous price range. Basically, the market jumps over the resistance/support and trades higher/lower without stepping into that gap. Imagine that you own stock ABC, which has been trading between 22 and 28 for the past few months. One day, you look at the price of the stock and are startled to notice that it is now trading at 32. What happened here? When you check the action of the day you notice that the stock opened at 30 and traded up to 33 before settling the day at 32. What you have noticed is a breakaway gap. Perhaps the resistance of 28 just gave way and the market opened at 30. As long as this stock stays above the new support zone of 30, the breakaway gap will be viewed as a very bullish event. Should the stock trade back into the gap and close that gap, it will be viewed as negative for that security.

A *runaway gap* is the other gap in the same chart. This gap merely signifies that the market is exceedingly bullish/bearish and is continuing the trend in place. The placement of this gap is usually found in the middle of the move; thus, you can expect to see further action in the direction of that trend. As with the breakaway gap, a close below this gap is negative/positive, depending on the direction of the trend.

On the floor, it is commonly believed that a second gap the next day in the same direction has the opposite effect. If we have one upside gap on the chart and trade higher, then have another upside gap the next day, it is considered to be a negative. This has been referred to as the double gap rule. As a futures trader, should we see two gaps in a row on two successive days, we would take the opposite position. For example, should the Russell 1000 gap open higher and stay above that gap, we would have a breakaway gap. If the next day the Russell 1000 gaps higher again, the futures trader would believe that the gap will not hold and would sell the futures to take advantage of the double gap rule. This rule works about 80 percent of the time. Typically, the second gap isn't considered a runaway gap because it is usually filled by the end of the trading session.

An *exhaustion gap* is found at the end of a move and, as advertised, it is a sign of exhaustion. This tells you that the move is over. An island reversal is created by two gaps in opposite directions, leaving what looks like an island on the chart.

HEAD-AND-SHOULDERS TOPS AND BOTTOMS

Head-and-shoulders tops and bottoms can be seen in charts when they are putting in a high or a low. There are three distinct moves to this formation that apply to both tops and bottoms. First let's examine a head-and-shoulders top (Figures 4.14 and 4.15). The first move we notice is nothing

FIGURE 4.14 Head-and-shoulders top. (Copyright © 2006 eSignal. Published by eSignal, www.esignal.com.)

FIGURE 4.15 Closeup of head-and-shoulders formation. (Copyright © 2006 eSignal. Published by eSignal, www.esignal.com.)

out of the ordinary; it is simply a move up with a reaction pullback. We then see a rally from the previous reaction pullback, which leads to a deeper or equal reaction pullback. The third part of the move is another rally, which fails to equal the two previous rallies. This leads to a reaction pullback that is somewhat deeper than the previous ones. We have now identified the right shoulder, head, and left shoulder. The reaction trough from the highs of the left or third shoulder rally attempt may break the neckline of the first reaction low and the second (head) reaction low. This is an ominous occurrence, leading to a sell signal (you can use a measured move, which can be found by drawing a vertical line from the peak of the head to the neckline; take that number and subtract it from the neckline and you have a projected target for the move). There is one more important ingredient for a perfect head-and-shoulders formation—that is, increased volume on the reaction dips with lighter volume on the rallies.

The inverse head-and-shoulders bottom is made in a similar fashion but is the mirror image of the topping pattern just described. (See Figure 4.16.) The first reaction to the downside leads to a bounce back; then there is another sell-off, leading to a lower low. There is a bounce from that level, nearing the first bounce seen. Again the market slides, but it stops before even matching the first low. The bounce from that low removes the necklines seen in the previous bounces. As the market moves

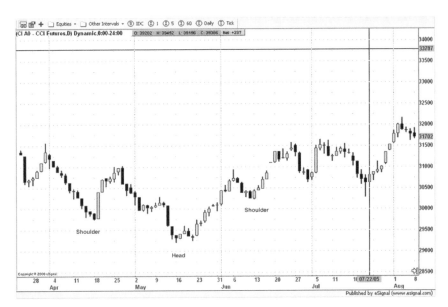

FIGURE 4.16 Head-and-shoulders bottom. (Copyright © 2006 eSignal. Published by eSignal, www.esignal.com.)

above the neckline, we have a good buy signal. The target may be measured much as was described in the head-and-shoulders top. We draw a vertical line from the bottom of the head to the neckline. We then add that distance onto the neckline number. Voilà! A target is found.

SAUCER BOTTOM

We on the floor call these formations a saucer or rounding bottom because a consolidation or sideways movement becomes the bottom. We notice that the lows begin, at a very gradual rate, to print slightly higher highs; they pause, then again make a mini-move to the upside. These patterns take a while to develop, but usually lead to a robust rally. As a day trader, I find that these patterns are visible on short-term charts and usually lead to the expected rally.

TEACUP BOTTOM

This formation is derived from the saucer bottom. After the rounding bottom formation, some backing and filling is seen, which looks like a cup's handle. This handle is a consolidation pattern, which eventually leads to the continuation of the rally. While this formation isn't usual, it is a valuable formation that seems to work, both on intraday charts as well as on longer-term charts.

ROUNDING TOP

This is the opposite of a saucer or rounding bottom. It is seen as the market stalls at the top of a rally, seeming to go nowhere fast, then slowly but surely begins to give way to the downside. The resultant chart looks like a rounded hill. This is a valid sell signal.

FLAGS

There are several kinds of flags: a bull flag, a bear flag, and a pennant. It is easy to identify a flag by the polelike rally or retreat seen on the chart. See Figure 4.17 for an example. These formations are particularly useful for

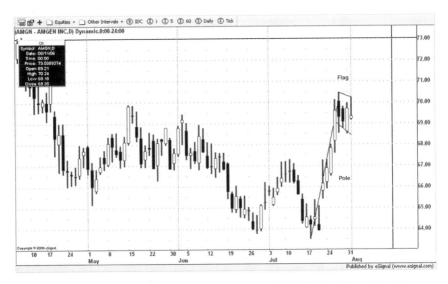

FIGURE 4.17 Flag. (Copyright © 2006 eSignal. Published by eSignal, www .esignal.com.)

day traders. Intraday charts lend themselves to these types of formations. It seems as though markets move in fits and starts; this is clearly seen on very short-term intraday charts. The pole or extreme rally/decline is usually followed by a period of consolidation, or backing and filling. This backing and filling period will be on declining volume. A flag is usually a continuation pattern. Why? Because it is generally a resting point or pause before the pattern continues. Some flags (bear flags) do signal that the trend will be reversing, but let us first deal with a continuation pattern (bull flags).

Bull Flag

With a bull flag formation, at the top of the pole there is a consolidating period when the market is backing and filling. The consolidation takes the form of a parallelogram or rhombus that looks like a flag tilting in the opposite direction of the pole (See Figure 4.18.) These patterns occur frequently in intraday markets and seem to be very reliable clues to the movement of the market under investigation. Should we have a pole to the downside and a flag at the end of that pole pointing in the opposite direction of the pole, it is telling us that the sell-off will continue.

FIGURE 4.18 Bull flag. (Copyright © 2006 eSignal. Published by eSignal, www .esignal.com.)

Bear Flag

With a bear flag formation, at the top of the pole we notice there is again a pause; however, this pause is different from that of the bull flag. The same consolidation is seen; however, this time the flag is pointing in the *same* direction as the pole. (See Figure 4.19.) This is not a continuation pattern, but rather a warning of an impending change of direction: in the case of a rally from up to down, and in the case of a sell-off from down to up. Again, these patterns are quite reliable and are frequently found on intraday charts.

Pennant

A pennant is a triangular formation that is found at the top of a pole. (Figure 4.20.) The distinct triangle is telling us that the market is getting narrower and narrower, getting ready to spring or unleash the coil in the direction of the previous pole. Volume becomes increasingly lighter. Pennants can be found in both up and down markets and are yet another continuation pattern.

FIGURE 4.19 Bear flag. (Copyright © 2006 eSignal. Published by eSignal, www.esignal.com.)

FIGURE 4.20 Pennant formation. (Copyright © 2006 eSignal. Published by eSignal, www.esignal.com.)

FIGURE 4.21 Wedge formation. (Copyright © 2006 eSignal. Published by eSignal, www.esignal.com.)

Wedge

The wedge formation (Figure 4.21) is similar to a pennant, except that instead of just getting a narrower range, the wedge also points in a direction. As the wedge proceeds, the volume becomes increasingly lighter, as is also true for the pennants.

M AND W REVERSAL PATTERNS

Reversal patterns are found at the top of a chart as well as the bottom of the chart. The M cannot be a bottom formation, and the W cannot be a top formation. You will find Ms only at the top and Ws only at the bottom. No ifs and/or buts on that one.

M Pattern

An M pattern can be found only at the top of a move. This is not a continuation pattern, but one that is a signal that the opposite direction will likely be the next move. It is a reversal pattern. See Figure 4.22 for an example of an M pattern.

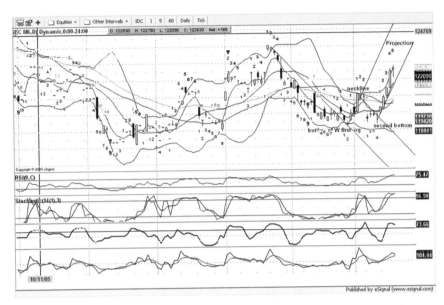

FIGURE 4.22 M pattern. (Copyright © 2006 eSignal. Published by eSignal, www .esignal.com.)

I frequently use the M pattern with great success. The first leg up, which may look like a pole, is made. A reaction and consolidation is seen from that high, which forms a trough. This is followed by another rally, preferably not as robust as the original one. Then, the market retreats to the bottom (the first reaction trough), which is broken. This is your sell signal! You can take a measurement of the possible target by measuring the distance moved on the first leg of the M, subtract it from the second top, and you have a target of the move. This is a very reliable pattern.

W Pattern

The W pattern is the opposite of the M pattern and is found at the bottom of the move. (See Figure 4.23.) Again, we are looking at a reversal pattern. There is a leg down, polelike or not; then a bounce from that level is seen, followed by another retreat, which is not as deep as the first one. As the rally continues from this level, the neckline of the W is removed, thus reversing the trend and giving you a buy signal.

FIGURE 4.23 W pattern. (Copyright © 2006 eSignal. Published by eSignal, www .esignal.com.)

INSIDE DAY AND OUTSIDE DAY

A lot of information can be gotten from these patterns. If the market fails to make a new high or new low and lacks that energy, you can determine something about that day's trading. These are terms that you will hear about and should know.

- *Inside day.* The entire range of the period under investigation is smaller than the range of the preceding period. If the range on one day is five points from high to low, an inside day that follows would be one where that high is never met and the low is not tested. The range would be smaller than the five-point range of the previous period, maybe four points or perhaps, more likely, three. In many instances when there is an inside day, energy may be building for the move that will follow.
- *Outside day.* The opposite of an inside day, an outside day is a picture of a trading period with a higher high and a lower low than the previous day saw. An outside day is also important because if there was a new high but the market closed below the previous low, that would be considered extremely ominous for the bullish viewpoint. By contrast, should the market print a new lower low, reverse from that low, and close at a higher high than the previous bar, that would be considered bullish. Get the picture?

CONCLUSION

Flags, Ws, and Ms are all reliable patterns that work on all time frames and with very good reliability. Saucers and teacups are also reliable, but usually a longer time frame is needed for these patterns to build. There are many thoughts about gaps, but it is my experience that most of them are filled. Usually, when stepping into a gap, the trade is magnetized into the hole, which it will partially fill. Within a day or so, the entire gap will be filled. Head-and-shoulders tops are not as reliable as they are advertised to be; however, head-and-shoulders bottoms *are* reliable. Go figure! As a trader, I like Ws, Ms, and flags, but then, of course, my time frame is much shorter than that of the average trader, unless I have an options position on; then, it can take years to unwind (well, maybe not years).

CHAPTER 5

Momentum and Other Indicators

S ome traders believe that all momentum indicators and oscillators work. In truth, I do not find this to be so. I restrict their use to just three or four such indicators for my work applications and for trading. The cold fact is that in use you'll have to find the indicators that work best for you and your needs and then stick to those indicators.

In my experience, the classic stochastic indicators lag behind the market. To keep up, I choose to use fast stochastics. I find that the Relative Strength Index (RSI) default levels don't work; for my purposes, I have changed them to 9 periods rather than stay with the 14-period default level. Stochastic oscillators, the Relative Strength Index (RSI), and Bollinger bands will be briefly discussed at the end of this chapter. These indicators are frequently used and often referred to by analysts and the press alike.

SIMPLE MOVING AVERAGES

Moving averages are self-explanatory: They define the average of a quantity of some item that is subject to alteration, reflecting the most current available data. Basically, a moving average is an average that moves. What does this mean to us? Take a 10-period simple moving average and compile that average. In such an example, where we have just decided how many periods we are going to average, we'll do that 10-period moving average of a stock and, to simplify the math, we're going to trade in whole numbers. We will start with the past 10 days' closing prices on a security (say, XYZ Company):

Day 1	90
Day 2	92
Day 3	89
Day 4	88
Day 5	87
Day 6	89
Day 7	91
Day 8	91
Day 9	92
Day 10	90
Total	899

Now divide by 10 days; your moving average is 89.9.

Day 1 will be dropped on the eleventh day of trading, when the price is 91; so the day 1 number is now 92 and day 10 is now 91. The total sum of these numbers is 900. Divide that by 10 and your moving average is now 90. Getting the picture?

Why use moving averages? To smooth out the trading picture and to show a definite trend pattern; this is a trend-following indicator. It is also, by its very construction, a backward-looking protocol that can be quite useful. You can easily program it into your computer, or simply do it longhand. It is clearly easy to do. How can it help you in your examination of the market? By utilizing a moving average study, you will be able to readily see a change in direction. Be advised that the longer the moving average study is, the less sensitive it will be to the swings of the market. And the shorter the moving average study is, the more spiky it will be. For example, a 200-day moving average will be a lot flatter than a 50-day moving average or a 10-day moving average. Which brings us to an interesting use of a succession of moving averages.

It should be noted that most moving averages are calculated from the closing prices of the subject stock; however, you could just as easily use the *average* price of the day's trade. Such a calculation is made by averaging the open, the high, the low, and the close and using that number instead of the closing price. This approach gives a more accurate reading. As a futures trader I regularly use the open, the high, the low, and the close to arrive at an average number. For even more accuracy, you might also weight your figures by volume at price points.

Once these numbers have been plotted on the chart of a security you're checking, you can easily see the trend of the market. Further, you can visualize that when the market trades below that moving average number, it will likely have negative implications. Remember that the longer the look-back period, the less the effect of current data on the moving average.

LINEARLY WEIGHTED MOVING AVERAGE AND EXPONENTIAL MOVING AVERAGE

We have completed our discussion about a simple moving average. Let us now address two more kinds of moving averages that are in use: linearly weighted moving average and exponential moving average. Both of these measures attempt to make the current data more important than the older data by assigning more weight to the current data. I use exponential moving averages because the moving average uses all the data available to it. With the linear moving average each day is assigned a value for the lookback period; the most recent data is given the most weight. The exponentially smoothed moving average also gives the most weight to the most recent data and—without giving you the formula, which is complicated—seems to combine the best of both the simple moving average and the linearly weighted moving average.

Rather than go through the math involved in calculating these measurements, most market software has programmed the formulas. (If you are interested in understanding the underlying formulas, John Murphy's book, *Technical Analysis of the Financial Markets* (John Wiley & Sons, 1999) provides that information.) What would I use? Well, if I were to use only one moving average, it would be a five-period exponential moving average. Remember, however, I prefer to trade on both an intraday basis as well as on a longer-term basis. My rule is that should the five-period exponential moving average reside under the current price, a long position might be the choice; should the five-period exponential moving average be above the price of the subject under investigation, a short position would be in order. Do I use this in isolation? Absolutely not!

What can we do about correcting for the spikiness of the short-term moving average? Add another moving average that is longer. That approach lets you create a moving average convergence/divergence (MACD). The MACD describes the behavior of averages, moving together and then diverging, one going in a different direction from the other. These divergences can lead you to note a change in trend; they are useful in identifying spots of strength or spots of weakness.

The longer a moving average is, the flatter it will appear because it has incorporated all the trades (for whatever number of days back) you might be looking at. Typically, 200-day and 50-day moving averages are used by portfolio managers, but not by traders unless they are looking for support at very sensitive levels, like the 50-day moving average.

As mentioned earlier, when compiling the moving averages, it is customary to use the closing price for the day's trade. A better number would be derived by using the average of the open, the high, the low, and the close of the day. Perhaps even better than that might be a volume-adjusted average for the day's trading session. This number would be adjusted to give more weight to the prices with the heavier volumes. I haven't seen this done, but it does have merit from a trading point of view.

It is commonly accepted that should the price of the subject under review move below the moving average, this action would signal a change of direction. This means if the moving average is at 42 and the stock has been trading at 43 and then drops to 41, an ominous change might be brewing. This moving average will be viewed as an area of support that failed to support the market. Further, it is negative for the subject to trade below the moving average.

The moving average can be support *or* resistance. If the market is above the moving average it could be a bullish sign, but when trading below the moving average, a bearish view might be appropriate. I use the moving average in just that manner. Remember, I am a very short-term trader in most instances. I use violations of these markers as warnings of the possibility of a trend reversal. Just as I use the short-term moving averages, I also enjoy using the longer-term averages. Because they are of a longer term, they are more important should they be violated.

I use exponential moving averages because they do not give equal weight to each piece of data; rather, they place more importance on the most recent data. Therefore, the moving average is more sensitive. There is nothing wrong with an equally weighted moving average, especially when using a short-term study, but it is my preference to use the exponentially weighted moving average. (If I could get it weighted as to the volume, I would prefer that above all.) The shorter the moving average, the spikier the line and the more false signals will be generated. The bottom line is that you have to experiment to see which moving average works best for you.

The longer averages remove some of the noise of the market. Noise refers to trades that create false data, cross-trades (a buy and sell by one broker), and so forth. They also work well in identifying trend reversals. The downside is that they are too slow to be usable unless you want to identify long-term support or resistance.

With crossover moving averages, usually described as MACD, you create two moving averages, one short-term and one longer. As the shorter moving average crosses the longer moving average, you get a signal. It could be to the upside or to the downside. It is the cross that counts. Typically 5 and 20 days are paired, 10 and 50 periods are paired, and 50 and 200 periods are paired. These lines are plotted on a graph and give you buy and sell signals. You might opt to plot them on a histogram. Either way, they tell you the same thing. If we have a moving average crossover and a trend line violation in the chart, we have an extremely strong signal.

It is possible to use envelopes around the moving average in an effort to define where you believe the upside and downside might be found. Simply take your moving average and add either 3 percent or 5 percent bands around that average and use those numbers for possible support and resistance areas. I don't use them; I use Bollinger bands.

BOLLINGER BANDS

Bollinger bands plot two standard deviations above and below the moving average, which is normally 20 periods long. (See Figure 5.1.) Standard deviation is a statistical measurement that delineates 90 percent of the probable movement of the trade; thus, this is an important measurement, and one that I use daily. These bands not only show you where 95 percent of the trade is likely to be, they also indicate volatility. Once the trade is at

FIGURE 5.1 Bollinger bands on natural gas chart. (Copyright © 2006 eSignal. Published by eSignal, www.esignal.com.)

the upper or lower edge of the band, it usually can't stay there very long and will back away from the band.

These bands become very wide in volatile markets and very narrow in low-volatility markets. From a trader's viewpoint, it looks as though the bands are a jaw around the moving average when the volatility is low. It is also a good indicator of impending moves. These bands do not stay wide nor do they stay narrow for very long, but rather move with the trade, getting wider and then narrower.

RELATIVE STRENGTH INDEX AND STOCHASTICS: AN OVERVIEW

J. Welles Wilder Jr. developed the indicator called the Relative Strength Index (RSI), which was first introduced in 1978. His index measures the strength of one market versus another market, say IBM versus the S&P 500. This measurement tells the user if the subject is doing better or worse than another subject. Today, we generally use the S&P 500 as the benchmark for the market.

The stochastic indicator is a product of George Lane. This indicator is a mathematical formula that plots a fast line calculated from a formula measuring the closing price in relationship to the issue's range of a period of time, usually five days, against a second line that is just a three-day smoothed average of the former line. What is important is not the formula but your ability to use said formula in making decisions. You are looking for the fast line to cross over the longer line, signaling a change in direction and giving you a buy or sell signal. The formula renders readings from 0 to 100 percent. You can use the exponential or the raw calculation. I strongly suggest that you use the exponentially smoothed calculation. This oscillator also measures overbought and oversold conditions.

Figure 5.2 shows a stochastic indicator and RSI indicator on a chart.

I do use them for day trading and as useful tools for option strategies. To help me make my decisions I also use the 9-period RSI and some of the systems devised by Thomas DeMark that are described in his book *The New Science of Technical Analysis* (John Wiley & Sons, 1994) in which he uses lower lows or high highs, which he counts when compared to, say, four days earlier. This begins his counting, which, after a number of consecutive downs or ups, may issue a buy or sell signal. This is worth looking into, although it has been my experience that the count varies according to the product traded. Some will issue a buy or sell after, say, a 9-count, whereas, sugar recently went to 24 before we felt the sell. There is another indicator that I will share with you; it has no name but is one I

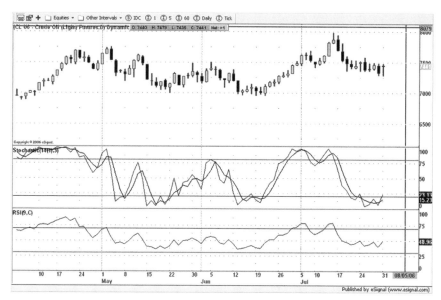

FIGURE 5.2 Stochastic indicator and RSI indicator on crude oil. (Copyright © 2006 eSignal. Published by eSignal, www.esignal.com.)

developed in the early 1990s. I simply use the Commodity Channel Index (CCI) with a 5-period exponential moving average over it. As the moving average line crosses the CCI line, I get either a buy or a sell signal. It is useful because it gets you into the trade in a timely fashion and keeps you there until there is a reasonable change. This indicator is described in the Appendix.

CONCLUSION

The moving average can be used and formatted to your own needs and desires. It is a useful tool to identify the trends and to keep you on the correct path. Many traders combine both short and long moving averages to create a trigger. That seems to work well, but I also like Bollinger bands, which work extremely well. You can use as many moving averages as you desire, but remember, if you crowd your chart you will have chaos and confusion. Keep your charts simple and easy to understand. I also find it useful to keep my indicators and studies the same on all the markets that I follow. Why? So I don't have to take time trying to figure out where something is and what I was using and possibly thinking about.

CHAPTER 6

Bonds, Currencies, and Commodities

In this chapter, I will first attempt to explain bonds. Government bonds trade more than any other security and are highly liquid. They can be bought at any time and sold with the same ease as the purchase. There are many differences among bonds. Here I try to clear up the bond fog and explain some important classification differences. Remember, this is a brief overview of bonds, not the bible of bonds. That bible can be found in *The Handbook of Fixed Income Securities*, Seventh Edition, edited by Frank J. Fabozzi with Steven W. Mann (McGraw-Hill, 2005).

Currencies play a more important role in our marketplace every day. This role will only increase with time as we have become a global economy. Today, we rely on other countries for much of the production and outsourcing of products. Because the world does not have a single currency to unify it, we trade in many currencies. This currency risk must be assessed and removed for trading with our partners.

Commodities have become an important asset class. This recently revived asset class is negatively correlated to the securities market. Commodities as an asset class should be a part of any balanced portfolio. We will briefly discuss commodities. As a commodity floor broker/hedger/trader, I will let you take a look at my world from inside the ring.

BONDS

The purchase and sale of bonds far exceed the market activity in any other type of security. The bond market, and more specifically the government bond market, is a huge market, from repurchase agreements (repos) to 100-year bonds, from overnight to decades-long durations. These instruments alone are worthy of a comprehensive text. In an effort to simplify this complex topic, I will begin by trying to answer some of the most general questions bearing on an understanding of bonds and other bondlike securities: What are bonds? What are convertible bonds? How do they differ from stocks? We will here discuss yield, maturity, taxes and other subjects that are bondlike in nature. It may not qualify you as an expert, but you will be able to confidently trade this class of assets.

So What Are Bonds?

Bonds are the most traded asset class in the world. Why? Because they offer fixed income and possible appreciation. Depending on their quality can be used for good faith margin and their returns, bonds can reduce the cost of borrowing. For example, if you had a bond with a 10 percent yield and the broker loan rate was 12 percent, you would have a cost of 2 percent. Of course, it isn't as clean as all that: There are some haircuts and only 90 percent of the bond is usable, and there is the marked-to-the-market stuff. But in theory it works this way. What the bond investor gives up for safety is the growth and appreciation of equities. If you lend money, you can get your money back (usually); but if you are an owner, there is no limit to the growth you can enjoy (only in a good market).

A purchase of a bond is a loan of money. In return, the investor is paid interest for lending the money, much as a bank might receive interest when you make a mortgage. You, as the buyer of the bond, lend the money. It is said that "you can loan or you can own."

Types of Bonds

There are many different kinds of bonds, even overnight and 100-year bonds. These are a bit out of the ordinary for the average investor, but they do exist. Disney issued a 100-year bond to help with the funding of Euro Disneyland in the early to mid-1990s. We have government securities: notes with maturities up to several months and bonds with maturities up to 30 years. We have agency issues, as well as corporate bonds, which may or may not be secured. We have municipal bonds, mortgage-backed bonds, asset-backed securities, convertible bonds, convertible preferred, preferred, international bonds, dollar-denominated bonds, and non-dollar-denominated bonds. Money markets are made up of bonds that are very short-term and usually not backed by anything.

International bonds that are issued by foreign entities can be separated into two distinct types: dollar-denominated and non-dollar-denominated bonds. A dollar bond will pay interest in U.S. dollars, whereas a foreign bond that is a non-dollar-denominated bond will pay interest in the currency indicated on the indenture of the bond. For example, if you buy a non-dollar-denominated bond issued by the United Kingdom, it will pay you interest in pounds sterling. If you buy a dollar-denominated bond issued by the United Kingdom, it will pay you interest in U.S. dollars. Bonds issued by a foreign nation that trade here in the United States are called "Yankee bonds." These bonds trade in the United States but are not issued here; they are foreign bonds that are being traded here. Eurodollar bonds are bonds denominated in dollars, traded outside the United States.

CARs and CARDs   Certificates for automobile receivables (CARs) and certificates for amortizing revolving debts (CARDs) are asset-backed securities, or bonds backed by real assets. There are railcar-backed bonds, boat-backed bonds, computer-backed bonds, accounts receivable, and Small Business Administration loans. All of these loans enjoy a degree of safety because there is a hard asset backing the bond.

Treasury Notes   Treasury bonds are sold at a discount and reach full value at maturity, which is under a year; these instruments are called notes. They are backed by the full faith and credit of the U.S. government.

Treasury Bonds   Treasury bonds are sold at auction and have coupons. They have maturities of from 1 year to 30 years, and interest is paid on the bonds semiannually. These instruments are backed by the full faith and credit of the U.S. government.

Yield or Coupon Bonds   Many bonds are issued with coupons attached, or an agreement by the borrower to send interest payments to the lender. A coupon may not be the yield on the bond. This isn't a trick statement. A yield identifies the return the investor can expect to receive for the loan of money. The coupon is the stated interest payment on that bond, based on par, which is quoted as 100 (this really stands for $1,000).

Therefore, if a bond is selling for less than par, say 90 ($900) and the coupon stated is 10 percent, you are getting a yield of more than 10 percent. For the year, you would get $100 (10 percent of par) but if you had paid only $900 for the bond, you are making more than 10 percent; your $100 yield will be 11.11 percent of $900. However, if you paid 120 for the bond ($1,200), your yield is much less: 8.33 percent of $1,200. The yield can be defined as the return you can expect to receive, based on the cost. Should you pay 120 for a bond, you still will get only 100 at maturity. Why? Because that is the amount that has been borrowed. You are paying a premium for a bond to get a better yield; you are paying more than the value of that bond at the time of redemption so that you can receive the coupon payments, which are higher than the current rate. It is the tax-free cash flow attached to that bond or loan that you want to capture. U.S. government bonds are not taxable by states, but are taxable by the federal government. Why buy a certificate of deposit (CD), which has penalties for early redemption, when you can buy a Treasury note or bond and sell it at any time and not have to pay state tax?

Premium Bonds   Premium bonds are bonds sold for more than they will be redeemed for. Why would you buy a premium bond? You would buy it for the cash flow of the coupon. Because the coupon is paying a higher rate than the current rate, the price of the bond is increased to adjust the yield of the bond to what an equivalent bond would be paying. For example, say you bought a noncallable bond with a 10 percent coupon at par about 15 years ago. At that time the current interest rate paid was 10 percent; the bond was AAA and safe. Today, bonds are yielding 5 percent. Do you think that a bond with a 10 percent coupon should be priced the same as a bond with a 5 percent coupon? The answer is obviously no; therefore, the buyer of the bond with the 10 percent coupon is willing to pay more for the bond to capture that 10 percent coupon. That bond will be a premium bond. The buyer wants the higher cash flow and is willing to pay more than the bond will be worth at maturity, which will be par, to capture that income.

Discount Bonds   Discount bonds sell for less than they will be redeemed for. These bonds are subject to capital gains tax if held to maturity.

All bonds can be subject to capital gains tax if they are sold for more than they were bought for. You can use a loss for bonds, sold at a loss. There is a footnote on that one. If you paid more than the bond is worth, or more than par, you cannot declare that as a loss on redemption at par. Had you bought the bond at par and sold it for less than par, it would be a bookable loss. At the end of every year, we do bond swaps. We literally trade our losing bonds, book those losses, and buy similar bonds to replace those bonds. We have created a loss on the books that is realized, but have used the money to buy very similar bonds to replace the liquidated ones. Our position doesn't really change, but we have created a tax loss. Many times, it is possible to upgrade your bonds when doing this.

Zero Coupon Bonds   These bonds are sold at a deep discount from the value of the bond at maturity. They pay no current interest rate. U.S. savings bonds are issued in a like manner. There are tax obligations due on those bonds for accrued interest and they must be paid. Sometimes Treasury bonds are stripped of their coupons and sold as zero coupon bonds, but they are called strips. Zero coupon bonds are issued by corporations, governments, and municipalities. These bonds have more risk, when compared to like securities with coupons. Why? Because there is no coupon to offset the interest rate risk on the bond.

American versus Foreign Bonds There is a basic difference between U.S. bonds and foreign bonds. U.S. bonds, whether corporate or municipal (if not zeros), pay interest semiannually. Foreign bonds may, in many cases, pay interest on an annual basis. When calculating the return, one must adjust that information for comparing bonds. Bonds are identified by their maturity and the coupon. For example, if I ask for a New Jersey Turnpike 3.5 of September 2020, I am asking about a bond with a coupon rate of 3.5 percent, due in September of 2020. That is how I identify the issue. Nowhere have I identified the price of that bond. The bonds will be quoted, removing a zero. Example: A bond may be 90, bid at 90.12; English translation is: 900, bid at 901.2.

Maturity of a Bond

It is understood when purchasing a bond that it has a definite maturity date in the future, but there are other conditions that may be stated on the face of that bond. If the bond has a call feature or a put feature, it must be stated in the indenture of that bond. If the bond has a sinking fund feature, this must be stated. These conditions affect the pricing of that bond. Should the bond be insured as to coupon and payment, this is reflected in the price of the bond. Insurance can be an add-on or come with the issuance. The insurance can be for the principal (the loan or face value of the bond) or can be for both principal and interest. Of course, when you add interest as well, you will make that bond really safe and you will reduce the income you are to be paid because you have removed both the principal risk and the reinvestment risk of that bond. The safer the bond is, the less interest the borrower must pay to the lender. Thus, a bond that is insured for both the coupon and the principal will pay the investor less than a bond without any insurance.

Back to the maturity of the bond: A call feature will affect the maturity of the bond.

Callable Bond With a callable bond the borrower has stated that it may call the bond early, or before maturity, and it states what, if any, premium will be paid for this early redemption. For example, a bond could be issued with a 10 percent coupon, due in 2036, callable in September of 2016 at 101. The interpretation is that this bond is a 10-year bond, callable at 101 at the issuer's discretion. Thus, when we price this bond, it is priced as though it would be called in 10 years, allowing the issuer to pay a smaller coupon (lower cost to the issuer). This bond reflects interest rate risk for the buyer who wants to lock in the rate for 30 years. Why? Because after only 10 years, the issuer can pay off the loan, leaving the lender with his cash back in his pocket. You might say: So what? It is a big deal, though, when you have to reinvest that money and the rates are no longer where they were; thus, the buyer of a callable bond is subject to interest rate risk.

Puttable Bond   The buyer of the puttable bond has purchased a bond with the provision that he may sell that bond back to the issuer at a time prior to the maturity of that bond. Usually, that bond's put window is limited, and the provision must be exercised within that window, or that window will close.

Short-term bonds are bonds with maturity dates up to 5 years, intermediate bonds mature in from 5 to 12 years, and long-term bonds have maturity dates of 12 to 30 or more years.

Duration   This is a measure of volatility in the price of a bond or fixed income security. (The reason I adjusted that to fixed income security is that preferreds will fall in that group, as well.) In *The Handbook of Fixed Income Securities*, Third Edition, edited by Frank J. Fabozzi (Business One, 1991, p. 124), the definition of duration is given as: "First formulated by Frederick Macaulay in 1938, duration is a weighted average term-to-maturity of the security's cash flows. The weights are the present values of each cash flow as a percent of the present value of all cash flows (i.e., the weights are the present value of each cash flow as a percent of the bond's full price)."

Bonds have a 360-day year.

When you buy a bond, you pay accrued interest on that issue. The previous holder of the bond is paid interest for the time he owned the bond. That is calculated and would appear on the sales slip; for example, price of the bond, 90, plus accrued interest. That interest payment will come back to the purchaser after the coupon payment is made. Then, when the purchaser is paid his interest rate, it will be for six months and he will be paid back the accrued interest he paid out, when purchasing the bond.

Things that affect your bond are:

- Interest rates.
- Time to maturity.
- Inflation.
- Credit risk.
- Duration.
- Currency risk.

As interest rates go up, your bond will go down in value. The longer the maturity of the bond, the more interest rate changes will affect the price of the bond. Inflation is the enemy of all fixed income investors; as inflation rises, the fixes to prevent inflation will negatively affect the price of the bond, thus causing a loss, especially on the long end of the bond scale. The riskier the borrower is, the more it will have to pay to borrow money. There are measures to evaluate the risk of a bond, and one of these measures is called duration. Of course, there is always currency risk for those investing in Eurobonds.

Repurchase Agreement (Repo) and Reverse Repo

A repurchase agreement is usually done between dealers or banks, when one has no need for the security for margin and the other has a temporary need for security paper. A dealer will sell his excess securities to an investor with the simultaneous contract or agreement to repurchase those securities on a future date, at a specified price (which naturally will be higher).

The reverse repo is the exact opposite of the repo situation where the dealer and the individual enter into a contract to sell and repurchase the securities. In this reverse repo instance, the dealer is the buyer and the individual is the seller. Remember, the owner of the paper, whether for overnight or for two days, is entitled to interest payment on that loan.

Some Other Kinds of Bonds That Are Commonly Traded

Sinking fund bonds require the issuer to retire a certain amount of the issue at specified dates.

Floating rate bonds have variable rates, which may be pegged to some interest rate like the London Interbank Offered Rate (LIBOR) or the Treasury bill rate. There are some floating rate bonds that reset every specified time period at a rate keyed to the current rate.

Variable rate bonds are bonds that have more than one coupon rate. For example, you could have a return of 8 percent for the first 10 years and then 9 percent thereafter, up to maturity.

Accrued Interest Calculation

Accrued interest (AI) is equal to the face value of bond, times coupon rate divided by 2 because there are two payments per year in American bonds (there is only one in a European bond unless otherwise stated), multiplied by the number of days from the previous coupon date to settlement date, divided by the number of days from the previous coupon date to the next coupon date:

$$AI = \left(FV \times \frac{c}{2} \right) \frac{d}{CP}$$

$$\text{Current yield} = \frac{\text{Yearly interest}}{\text{Current price}}$$

$$\text{Coupon} = \frac{\text{Yearly interest}}{\text{Par(100)}}$$

Current yield may be different from coupon rate. Bonds are priced to the call date, rather than to maturity, so that the investor can see the worst-case scenario. This, of course, is no guarantee that the call will be elected, but rather, is a risk that is being disclosed.

A zero coupon bond will always have a pure yield curve because there are no coupons. It also has the greatest risk because there are no coupons.

Municipal Bonds

Municipal bonds are debt securities that are issued by states and local governments. These issues generally enjoy exempt status from both state and federal income taxes. (There has been an issue, however, brought by two investors in Kentucky, challenging the taxability of the interest income on state bonds from other states.) Municipal bonds, in general, because of their tax-free status, pay less interest to the owners of these securities. For example, if you buy New Jersey state general obligation (GO) bonds, the interest paid on those bonds will not be subject to tax by either the state of New Jersey or the Internal Revenue Service (IRS).

The challenge brought by two investors in Kentucky was against the state of Kentucky, which found that out-of-state bonds were subject to state income tax. This is the case in every state that has a state income tax, with the exception of Kentucky . . . so far. The case was lost by the state of Kentucky, but is being appealed. Should the challenge stand, it would open the door in other states for investors to challenge the taxability of out-of-state bonds. For example, as a New Jersey resident, if I bought a tax-free bond issued by Kentucky, I would have to pay state income tax to New Jersey on the income received from that investment. True, it would remain federally tax free.

Not all municipal bonds are tax exempt; they must apply for that status, bond by bond. There are different types of municipal bonds. Some are general obligation (GO) bonds, which are backed by the state. Some are hospital bonds, backed by a hospital. Some are housing bonds, backed by housing. And so on. Each bond is assessed by the issuer's ability to pay that loan. The best rating will be awarded to insured bonds. All of these bonds have a legal opinion stated in the indenture. This is the part that tells you how safe these bonds are and what they are backed by, also, the opinion indicates whether the bond is a qualified tax-exempt bond.

Notes

Notes are municipal bonds with a term of three years or less. They are, by nature, short-term bonds. They can be for from just days to just a few years; usually, at most, about a year. These are issued in several categories and are viewed as a modality for temporary funding; they are: a bond anticipation note (BAN), a short-term fix until the anticipated bond is issued; a revenue anticipation note (RAN); and a tax anticipation note (TAN). All of these issues are short-term loans.

Convertible Bonds

These are hybrid securities; they are part bond and they could be part equity. They are classified as debt securities, but they have an equity kicker. These are bonds that will convert into the stock of the underlying company, provided that certain prior qualifications have been met. For example: A convertible bond may have a conversion rate of 20 shares per bond. That bond may have an exercise date and a call date; all terms of the conversion will be spelled out in the indenture of that bond on its face. If the bond is convertible into, say, 20 shares of a stock and par is equal to $1,000, then the buyer has the right to convert the bond into 20 shares of stock at $50 per share.

Let's go further: Say that Google issued a convertible bond that would pay the holder a 3 percent coupon for a term of 20 years with the right to convert that bond into 10 shares of Google. When Google issued this convertible bond, the stock was selling at $85 and it was not anticipated that it would go to $100 per share. (Of course, we are making up numbers here, but the buyer of the bond anticipated that the stock would rise, but was skeptical enough to not accept a no-dividend-paying stock and opted for the interest-paying hybrid, the convertible bond.) Thus, the bondholder is paid a 3 percent coupon while the common stockholder is being paid nothing; the stock does not pay a dividend. The bondholder has ownership in a hybrid security, called a convertible bond because it can be converted into equity.

Until that stock crosses the $100 per share mark, the bond will trade like a bond, but once the equity passes the $100 mark, that bond no longer behaves like a bond; rather, its value goes up in tandem with the stock's—perhaps not quite as much, but it goes up, nonetheless. Why? Because at that level of $100 per share the convertible bond acts like the underlying stock. Remember, 10 shares per $1,000 bond equals $100 per share; thus, the convertible bond is now an interest-paying stock and will act like the equity.

Suppose Google borrowed the money because it felt it needed to have more cash on hand to fund its needs and that 3 percent was a cheap loan. It therefore specified that it can call this bond in five years. The holders of the bond cannot convert the bond into stock until the designated time (exercise date).

There may come a time when Google wants to retire this debt from its balance sheet and, because it has a call provision, it may do so at the designated time (five years). Meanwhile, the bond will appreciate because the stock is trading at over $300 per share. It will trade along with the common stock and behave like a stock, rather than a bond.

Convertible Preferreds

Convertible preferreds are another type of hybrid security. Because they are preferred, they appear as equities; however, they are more associated with bonds in that they are perpetual bonds with no expiration date, unless stated otherwise. These preferreds also have an equity kicker because they are convertible into the common stock. As a preferred holder, it is typical practice that you have no voting rights. You do have a favored status with regard to a claim against the company; should that company be liquidated, you stand ahead of the common stockholders, but not the bondholders. Preferreds have a fixed dividend and may have been issued at par, but in this case, par is $100 per share, not $1,000. This dividend is at risk should the company fall upon bad times, and could be omitted without sending the company into default on a bond issue.

Cumulative Preferreds

Like convertible preferreds, cumulative preferreds are preferred issues that are perpetual bonds, but these issues have a special kicker in them. Should the issuing company omit a dividend on this preferred, the omitted dividend will accrue until such time as a dividend payment can be made, and then all the omitted dividends must be paid before dividends can be paid on the common stock of the issue. That is a really nice feature. I remember an issue called Galoob Toys that had such a cumulative preferred. It was a nice payday when that one paid off.

CURRENCIES

This group of financial instruments allows investors to buy or sell foreign currencies either in the cash markets or in the futures markets. These markets are used by banks for the most part, but also by businesses. Yes, individuals and corporations use this market either to speculate in or to hedge the currency risk their business or travel may expose them to. On the floor of the New York Board of Trade we have a ring full of speculators trying to buy cheap and sell expensive or sell expensive and buy cheap. Currencies can be in a single country, say the Japanese yen, or in currency pairs. Currency pairs are two currencies, one divided by the other: EUR/USD, USD/CAD, EUR/GBP, EUR/JPY, and so on. The price is a quote of the one currency in terms of another currency. For example, for the EUR/USD pair, 1.26 euros is equal to one U.S. dollar; for the GBP/USD pair, one U.S. Dollar will buy you 1.87 pounds sterling.

Many times, corporations like to have their risk of currency fluctuations removed by hedging in the futures arena. Today, the forex market has attracted many speculators. The market trades 24 hours a day, which offers the speculator an any time of day market. The forex market is an insomniac's dream.

Why would you be interested in trading a currency? It gives you the opportunity to take advantage of strong economies as well as weak economies by trading long the strong economy versus a short in the weak economy. Supply and demand are what determine the pricing. These currencies can be traded in open outcry as currency pairs or can be traded on Globex as single currencies. Interest rates, a country's economic health, sovereign risk, and growth all affect a currency's behavior.

At the New York Board of Trade, we trade currency pairs but mostly we trade the U.S. Dollar Index (USDX). It is an index because it is not only the U.S. dollar but rather a basket of currencies. The U.S. Dollar Index is a geometric average of six currencies versus the U.S. dollar. The currencies are the euro (57.6 percent), yen (13.6 percent), pound (11.9 percent), Canadian dollar (9.1 percent), Swedish krona (4.2 percent), and the Swiss franc (3.6 percent). When you buy the U.S. Dollar Index you are going long the U.S. dollar against the cited six currencies.

In addition to trading in these markets, currency hedging allows the exporter, importer, or those with currency risk to mitigate some of this risk. No, there isn't a perfect hedge; there never is, but currency hedging goes a long way in removing risk from the trade. Say you are IBM and have to sell your product in Europe and will receive euros rather than dollars for the sale. Do you really want to risk currency fluctuations? Perhaps it might be better to hedge that risk.

Options trade on this product, and therefore buying or selling an option might remove the risk of the trade for the set amount of time that trade is at risk.

COMMODITIES

This group of investments is the heart and soul of hard assets. We can break them into four main groups:

1. Metals (gold, silver, copper, aluminum, nickel, platinum, and palladium).
2. Agricultural commodities and meats (grain, cattle, hogs, soybeans, soy meal, soy oil, corn, and wheat).
3. Tropical commodities (coffee, sugar, orange juice, cotton, and cocoa).
4. Energy (crude oil, gasoline, heating oil, and natural gas).

We must not forget another group, which are the bonds, currencies, and financial futures. All of these assets and others make up that asset class called commodities. Why are commodities so important? Because they are negatively correlated with the stock market, which means that as the stock market goes up, this asset class will go down. A diversified portfolio absolutely requires some investment in commodities.

When you buy a commodity future (a forward contract), you are agreeing to buy the commodity at a certain time in the future. You are putting down a deposit on a future purchase. Therefore, you need but to put down as little as a few dollars on a contract that may be worth many dollars. For example, if you buy the December Russell 1000 futures contract, you have to put down a $10,000 deposit to control a contract that is worth more than $350,000. This contract will be delivered on the third Friday of December and it will settle in cash.

That is the first of many myths to be blown; you do not get a thousand stocks dumped on you in the third week of December. The contract settles for cash. For example, if you had bought the Russell 1000 for 700 and in December it closed at 800, you would have made 100 points. The basis for that calculation requires you to understand that each point is worth $500; therefore, 100 times 500 is what you would have made (i.e., $50,000). The contract's value in real dollars is the numerical value of the contract multiplied by 500 or divided by 2. So a contract that is trading at 700 is worth 700 times $500 or $350,000. You could take the 700 and divide it by 2, giving you 350 multiplied by 1,000 and you will have the same $350,000. That is what the contract is worth. If you took the appropriate weights of all 1,000 stocks in that contract, they would add up to $350,000. You could have lost a like amount, but unless you were sleeping you would have bailed out of that position. You would have sold the position before the $50,000 was lost. Or you could have bought the iShares IWB, which is the American Stock Exchange (AMEX) traded shares of the Russell 1000. Yes, you would have had to put up 50 percent of the cost; the same $350,000 exposure would have cost you $175,000 in margin. So, $10,000 versus $175,000; are you getting the idea? Of course, this leverage is also troublesome; therefore, your position will have to be monitored or hedged.

What have we learned? Futures are a deposit on a future purchase, which, no doubt, will be closed out before it ever comes near to due. Let us go on to sugar or coffee. Here are two of the softs that do not settle for cash. Yes, you will have the product if you don't pay attention and go to sleep while your clearinghouse is repeatedly warning you about "first notice day" along with other warnings of impending delivery. Should you want the delivery, you'll have to arrange for that delivery.

Long and Short Futures

If you buy futures, you are long the futures; if you sell the futures, you are short the futures. You don't have to ask permission to sell the futures, nor do you have to wait for an uptick. No, you just sell them and you are short. Why would you want to sell a futures contract? Well, say you are a farmer and you have planted corn that will be ready to harvest and deliver in 90 days. Wouldn't you like to sell the corn on the day it was planted to remove the price risk of that product? Futures allow you to do just that.

I am a speculator; I simply buy or sell what I think will make money for me. There is no reason for me to buy coffee unless I think it is going up in price. As a technical analyst, I look at the chart and decide that coffee is going to rally. I plunk down $800 to purchase a contract of coffee, and I am long. It is as easy as that. Every time coffee moves a point, I stand to lose or possibly gain $375 a point; so I watch what I am doing very carefully. Each commodity has its own margin rate, or good faith deposit. Each commodity has its own tick value; for example, the Russell indexes have a tick value of $25/.05 move; thus, .05 = $25. Cotton has the same tick value and a single-point move, say from 55.23 to 56.23, is worth $500. The USDX is $1,000/point and $10/tick.

Margin can be satisfied with a Treasury bill (T-bill) that will be put in your account as a good faith margin. Guess what: You earn interest while on margin; tell me, please, can you do that in the stock market? Yes, you can use a T-bill as margin in a stock account, but you will be charged a point or two above broker loan rate as margin interest. Say you use a bond with a 4 percent yield and the margin interest rate is 6 percent; you will be

paying 2 percent to borrow the money. In futures, you will get the 4 percent yield, and that is where the calculations end.

There are other things that set futures apart from stocks. The Russell
1000, 2000, 3000, S&P 500, and other futures contracts do not pay dividends as do the iShares or the exchange-traded funds (ETFs). You do
have an advantage over and beyond the leverage of the trade—that is, a
tax advantage. Whereas stocks held for a short term can be subject to ordinary income tax, futures have a different tax treatment. Futures, regardless of the holding period, will be treated as 60 percent long-term gain and
40 percent short-term gain. For me, that is a benefit.

Every futures contract has strict specifications and quantities. Coffee
graders determine which coffee beans are acceptable. The warehouses
where the coffee is stored are regulated. When you buy a contract of coffee on the New York Board of Trade, you are putting a deposit down on
37,500 pounds of washed Arabica coffee. There are specific months in
which this contract is traded. They are March, May, July, September, and
December. This contract will trade up to one business day prior to last notice day. First notice day is seven days prior to the first business day of the
delivery month. Last notice day is seven business days prior to the last
business day of the delivery month. There are specified delivery points,
say New York or New Orleans for example.

This reminds me of the time a few years ago when the January sugar
11 contract was expiring. There no longer is a January contract, and this
was the last one before that month was to be removed. For every contract
issued there is open interest. That can be described as positions that are
open and that will take delivery upon expiration. True, some contracts
such as the financials and even lean hogs settle for cash, but many contracts settle for the products. Most contracts are not delivered, as the
quality or other aspect of the product is not really wanted but rather used
as a method or removing price risk from the production equation. In this
instance of the final January sugar contract there were not enough out-
standing contracts of open interest to fill a ship. It takes 90 contracts to fill
a boat; each contract contains 112,000 pounds (50 long tons) of raw cen-
trifugal cane sugar. That may not sound important to you, but if you have
50 tons of sugar and need to get it from Brazil to the United States, and to
fill a boat you need 90 contracts, you will find yourself in a bit of a mess.
The ship costs could be $30,000 for transport and you are talking about
only a portion of a load to be transported.

It seems that some people did the math and figured out that there wasn't
enough open interest left in January sugar to fill a single boat. The smart
guys started to short January sugar, which was at 5 or 6 cents. They sold
and sold, then waited. The people who were long that contract needed to
unload their longs. Remember, the sugar couldn't be transported because it

was not economically feasible to do so. These smart traders offered to buy the sugar for a tick, which is 0.001 pennies per pound or $11.20 per contract. Yes, they bought it back for a tick and with that made tons of money, because they were smart enough to look at the open interest in that contract.

What occurred is history today but emphasizes the importance of looking at the open interest and delivery of the product. These rules of delivery are spelled out by each exchange with regard to the contracts that are traded on their floors. If you go to the New York Board of Trade web page you will see the rules of the road spelled out for you in very clear English. In the case of sugar, you have to move it. A delivery point for sugar is a port in the country of origin or "in the case of landlocked countries, at a berth or anchorage in the customary port of export." (www.nybot.com) For coffee, it could be deliverable in warehouses in a number of different states in the United States as well as Bremen/Hamburg, Antwerp, and other areas. One contract of coffee is 37,500 pounds with a tick worth 0.005 pennies per pound, which is $18.75 per contract or $375 per point. Each contract has its own peculiarity.

Futures Lingo

Backwardation. This occurs when the current month's price is higher than the months in the future. Say, May cocoa is selling for 14.00 and July is selling for 13.80; that is an example of backwardation.

Contango. This is what is normally expected to occur in the market such that each month, as you move farther away, is increasingly more expensive. There are storage costs, insurance, interest rates, and so on that are added to the value of the contract, thus making the longer-dated contracts more expensive. It is the exact opposite of backwardation, which, by the very word, tells you that things are backwards.

CTA. Commodity trading adviser.

Local. A floor trader who trades his own account.

Producer. An entity that needs to hedge its risks in the product.

Fund. A group of investors who are speculating in the commodity.

Hedger. A defensive player who finds price inefficiencies and takes advantage of them.

Arbitrageur. A form of a hedger who finds price inefficiencies in a pair of commodities that he will be long and short, offsetting the value of the other. For example, the Russell 1000 correlates well against the S&P 500; thus, if you buy the Russell 1000 at the New York Board of Trade (NYBOT) and sell the S&P 500 at the Chicago Mercantile Exchange (CME), you have put on a hedge. Sometimes they work better than at other times.

Limit moves. The terms *limit down* and *limit up* refer to predetermined levels at which trading will stop. For example, say cotton, which has a daily limit of 3 cents, opens the day at 55 and rallies to 58. That would be a limit move and you would not be able to buy or sell that contract over the 58 limit; however, you would be able to trade below the limit if someone would trade with you. Limit down works the same way. Many commodities have daily limits, whereas others do not have limits, such as coffee and sugar, to name two.

CONCLUSION

On the surface bonds may appear to be boring and very plain-vanilla, until you look at the ingredients. There are ways to invest in bonds taking advantage of their returns. Some bonds are secure and some aren't; some have equity kickers and some don't. Currencies are important, especially if you are interested in international trade or have a need to remove some of the risk involved using multiple currencies. You may say "No thanks," but just think about our neighbors to the north (Canada) and south (Mexico). We trade freely with these countries, and there is currency risk in doing so. The currency market allows investors to remove that risk from the equation. Perhaps not all the risk but enough risk can be removed so that the profit of the business can be insured.

Commodities also play a large role in removal of risk. Say you own an airline. Wouldn't you hedge your fuel risk in the commodity market, buying crude oil futures contracts to offset your future needs for fuel? This isn't done as speculation but rather to mitigate the possible fluctuations in the price of the commodity that could adversely affect your profits. If you are an airline, you are not speculating on fuel costs but paying a fixed cost that you can calculate now so that you can offset that risk. If your business is in airline transportation you want to make money on that part of the business. Hedging your fuel needs is simply good business sense.

PART II

Options Strategies

The options doctor is in and here to unwrap the mystery of options. As we have learned, the market is manic and moves with lightning speed both to the upside and to the downside. In this section of the book you will learn about options, an asset class that will help you with the ups and downs of your assets.

Regardless of the direction of the market, the Options Doctor will diagnose and treat the problem. Options Doctor is ready for patients!

We are going to be speaking about options, so naturally it is important that we define our terms and explain exactly what an option is. This is done in Chapter 7, which is a simple explanation of what people think is complicated. In Chapter 8 we try to use our newly learned skills to take advantage of a trending market, which could be up or down. In Chapter 9, we discuss how to deal with a market going nowhere fast and stuck in a range. Chapter 10 helps you understand what to do in a reversing market and how to take advantage of that market. So read on—it only gets better!

CHAPTER 7

Introduction to Options

This chapter is meant to give you the bare-bones guide to options. We will explore some of the terms and basically define options. Of course, when we speak of options we are speaking of puts and calls, both of which will be defined in a very easy-to-understand way. All you need to do is simple arithmetic—no logarithms or anything beyond eighth-grade math. If you found eighth-grade math difficult, just buy a cheap calculator and a pencil with a very large eraser.

Before we go on, it is important to understand that options are derivatives. As such, options depend on the pricing of the underlying asset. An option is akin to air, only it expires at some date and price certain in the future. It trades as an augmentation to something upon which it is priced. Owning an option on IBM that expires in January a year or even two years in the future is not like owning IBM the stock. It is an instrument that will be affected solely by the stock's price until the option expires. An option does not pay a dividend or have voting rights unless it is exercised. That action removes its classification as an option and changes it to that of a security or other issue. Either buying or selling an option is playing the game as the casino owner or the gambler coming in to play a hand of cards. As a derivative, options are priced and traded in direct relationship with the underlying issue. A derivative comes from something; in this instance that something is an asset, equity, futures contract, bond, or other security. That issue directly affects the price of the derivative either negatively or positively; therefore, it is a derivative, or derived from the issue. Think of it as an extension of a whole. You will see. Come on, open your mind and have fun with this extremely flexible asset class.

WHAT ARE OPTIONS?

Options are logical. The very word *option* indicates that you, the buyer, have a choice; that is precisely what options are. Succinctly, *options are instruments that allow a buyer or seller an opportunity to either presell or prebuy something.* This is a contract to perform and, as such, has both a stated future termination date and a sale price. The seller of an option has an obligation to do something, described in the contract; the buyer has free choice and is not obliged to do anything. Now, stated simply: If you buy something, it is yours to do with as you like. However, if you sell something, you are obligating yourself to some possible action as a consequence of that sale.

Why would an investor sell an option? One good reason is to receive payment for agreeing to an action at a future time certain. Why would an investor buy an option? Clearly, to purchase a privilege to either buy or sell something in the future.

The basic concept that if one sells something the seller is then obligated to do something is the key to understanding and having fun with options. When I say "having fun with options," I mean that using these derivatives allows the user to exercise creative and imaginative brain cells. It is like solving a Sudoku or a crossword puzzle. It provides for hours of fun. Say you are looking at your position and wondering what you can do to fix a problem or perhaps you have an opinion on the market. Well, options will afford you the opportunity to exercise that desire with a minimum of cash outlay. We have been told that "options are risky." Well, so is crossing the street. When used correctly, options are considered by many to be conservative instruments.

There are two classifications of options—calls and puts—but there are many different combinations of these two classifications you can use in your trading and investing. The next part of this chapter explains the ins and outs of calls and puts.

CALLS AND PUTS

A *call* is an option that permits the holder to buy something at a given time in the future and at a given price. As the holder of a call, you may "call it away." A *put* is an option that permits the holder to sell something at a given time in the future and at a given price. As a holder of a put, you may "put it to the seller." Immediately, you see that the holder of an option has the right to buy or sell something. This is a key concept in options transactions.

Here's an example. Let us say that you own a stock and that you would like to increase your return on that investment. Perhaps you might want to sell an option on that stock so as to increase its income return. The buyer of that option will have to pay you for the privilege with a pre-purchase price today, with expiry at some future date. That price is called the premium paid. Options premium payments are due immediately (within 48 hours) of the trade. You will receive the credit immediately. Options are not marginable; they are carried in your cash account. That statement is true of purchased options, but once options are sold or used in combination, they may have a margin consequence. Say you want to buy an item today; you don't have the funds to pay for it immediately but you know that you will have the money in two months. You ask the seller of the desired item to put that item on hold for your future purchase. The seller agrees but asks for a payment for keeping the item off the market for the next two months. You agree with the seller on a price, and there it is: You have entered into a contract with the seller to buy the item in two months at a preset date and at a price which you have already negotiated. For that, you are willing to pay a little extra money to keep your future purchase off the market. That is an example of a *covered call* or a *covered right*. Perhaps the best way to illustrate the details of such a transaction is to offer an example. Say you own 100 shares of stock in General Electric Company (GE). You will get your quarterly dividend and any appreciation generated by the increased value of that stock, but what else? Nothing! What *wasn't* mentioned was that you would also be at risk for the decrease in value of that stock, should the market take a spill.

How do you increase the income on that security (outside of day trading the security for intraday gyrations)? Now, there is a way to increase that income: that is, by preselling that stock. Actually, you are selling somebody the right to buy that stock from you at some set price, and subsequently that right expires at some set future time.

Let's say that you bought a stock for $30 per share and you own 1,000 shares. You will get your dividend, but you can also increase that income by selling a call against that stock ownership or, as they say, a *long position*. This is known as a *covered call write*—"covered" because you own the stock, "call write" because you have sold somebody the right to buy the stock from you (call the stock away from you) at some future date and you have received payment for selling this privilege. Yes, it is your money to do with as you like. You may choose to:

- Own GE @ $30.
- Sell GE January 2007 35 call for 2.10.

This example demonstrates that you are allowed to hold the stock until March, receiving December and March dividends; annual yield is 2.597

percent (see Figure 7.1 and Table 7.1). On the third Friday in March, if the stock is selling for more than $35, you will be obliged to sell that issue to the holder of that option for a price of $35 per share. Just to be clear about this: That obligation is filled from your account, if exercised, on the Monday following that expiration. If the stock is $60 it doesn't matter; you have agreed to sell those shares for $35 per share. For that presale, you were paid $2.10 per share when you sold the option. If the stock is selling for $25 per share, you still own the stock and can sell the option again (why would anyone pay $35 for a stock that is selling at $25?). Each option

FIGURE 7.1   General Electric covered call trade. (Copyright © 2006 eSignal. Published by eSignal, www.esignal.com.)

TABLE 7.1   Spreadsheet of GE Covered Call Trade

General Electric Company

Buy GE at $30/share	Debit $30/share	Debit 30 times 1,000	$30,000
Sell January 35 call	Credit 2.10	Credit $2.10 times 1,000	$2,100
December dividend	0.25 per share	Credit $0.25 times 1,000	$250
March dividend	0.25 per share	Credit $0.25 times 1,000	$250
Total		Cost	$27,400

is equal to 100 shares of stock, so if you own only 50 shares you can't do this. If you own 125 shares, you can sell one call.

This depicts a covered call. Generally, the call seller would be exceedingly happy if the stock owned did not fluctuate much. That would permit the continuation of this call-selling behavior.

The opposite side of buying a put or a call is selling a put or a call. When you sell something, you are obliged to *do* something. So, clearly, a sale of an option will force the seller to either sell or buy something, at a given price, at a given time. Options expire at a time certain in the future, and at a price certain in the future. When these instruments expire, they disappear forever.

Here is an example of selling a put and why this might be done. Let's say you love the stock of Home Depot Inc. (HD). This is a stock you would love to own but, right now, you feel that it is a bit pricey at $40.34. You wouldn't mind purchasing the stock for, say, $37.50 or so. What can you do with options to facilitate a purchase at that price? Obviously, if the stock doesn't fall to that level, you won't buy it; however, if you sell a put on HD for, say January 2007 with an exercise price of $37.50, you will receive $115 per option sold and have the chance, should the stock retreat, to purchase that stock at $37.50. In any case you will be paid for obligating yourself to that purchase. This transaction occurs in a margin account, inasmuch as you are promising to buy the stock at that price.

Home Depot current price: $40.34.

Home Depot 100 shares: $40.34 times 100 = $40.34.

Home Depot 1 37.50 January put: receive $1.15 or $115 for 100 shares.

Let's review the earlier example of buying a call. The General Electric January 2007 with an exercise price of 35 calls will cost you $2.10 or $210. This call will give you the right to purchase 100 shares of General Electric for $35 per share on the third Friday in January of 2007. This gives you control of $35 × 100 or $3,500 worth of stock for a mere $210. This is an example of leverage.

Following is an example of buying a put. (See Table 7.2) You own 1,000 shares of General Electric Company at $32 per share. You have some concern about the economy, but you don't want to sell your stock and would rather hold it at this time. You can purchase a put for the General Electric Company that will expire in the third week of January 2007 for a cost of $1.00 per share. Thus, for your $32,000 investment you can purchase insurance at a cost of $1,000 that will give you the right to sell that stock for $32.50 per share even if the market price is lower. That insurance policy expires in January 2007. Should the stock go down (e.g., to

TABLE 7.2 Spreadsheet of GE with Puts

General Electric Company

Buy 1,000 shares of stock	Cost		32.00	Debit	$32,000
Buy 10 January 32.50 puts	Cost		1.00	Debit	$ 1,000
		Cost per share	33.00	Cost of trade	$33,000

General Electric Company is 25 at expiration

Own 1,000 shares	Cost 32.00	Debit $32,000	Value of stock	$25,000
Own 10 puts	Cost 1.00	Debit $1,000	Value of option	$ 7,500
Result	Cost 33.00		Net value	$32,500[a]

General Electric Company is 60 at expiration

Own 1,000 shares	Cost 32.00	Debit $32,000	Value of stock at expiration	$60,000
Own 10 puts	Cost 1.00	Debit $ 1,000	Value at expiration	$ 0
Result	Cost 33.00	Debit $33,000	Value at expiration	$60,000[b]

[a]Net loss on trade is $500.

[b]Loss at expiration is on option purchase only. Trade generates $27,000 rather than $28,000 without option.

$25), you will have to ability to unload your holdings for $32.50 per share. However, should the stock go up to $60 per share, you do not benefit from the $1,000 you paid for insurance on your position.

HOW OPTIONS ARE USED

You might well have surmised that options are not just for equity traders; their applicability flows into bonds, futures, real estate—in fact almost any business instrument. In bonds, for example, many bonds are sold with a *call feature*. This feature gives the seller of the bonds (the borrower) the opportunity to redeem a held issue before maturity or pay off the loan in advance of the due date. You might ask why the seller would want or need that privilege. Consider this scenario: Let's say that you issued a bond some 10 years ago, a time when interest rates were double what they now are. Wouldn't it be a good business decision to resell that debt at a lower rate today, retiring the older higher-interest-rate debt? It is much like refinancing your home. Many bonds may have a call feature at par, which is

$1,000 per bond and quoted as 100. Some have a call feature that pays a little extra for calling the bond, say 101 or 102, which translates into $1,010 and $1,020 per bond.

Bonds may also have a *put feature*. This allows the holder (the lender) of the bond to be put, or redeemed, at a date or period of time before maturity. Maturity is the due date for a bond at which the loan matures and is due. With the put feature, the buyer of the bond can redeem this bond early, getting back all of the money lent without market risk. Why would that be so great? Well, if interest rates are rising quickly and the bond was issued with a low interest rate, before that rise in rates, the holder of the bond would doubtless appreciate the opportunity to relend the money at a higher rate.

To make this point clearer, let's say that 10 years ago you bought a house or condo and took out a 30-year fixed mortgage at a rather high rate, say 8 percent (an illustrative example), wouldn't you like the opportunity to pay off that high-interest-rate mortgage and replace it with a lower-interest-rate mortgage of, say, 6 percent? That is precisely what the issuer of bonds attaches to the indenture (rules of play on the face of the bond) at the time of issuance. Some bonds provide this feature and some do not, but if there is a call feature, it is required that it be clearly indicated to the buyer of the bond. Suppose banks could have a put feature (which they can't have) on a home mortgage. A bank could then put the mortgage back to the homeowner and refinance the home at a higher rate. Wouldn't they just love that one! Actually, many banks package and sell their loans in the open market to other institutions.

There are also options on land or real estate purchases. Say you want to buy a home, but your inheritance isn't due for another six months, after which time you will have the funds to pay for the purchase. You buy an option to purchase the property six months in the future at a given price. For that privilege, you pay the owner of the property a sum of money. That option locks up the price of the real estate for your purchase at or before that option expires. Should the option expire without your purchasing of the property, you would forfeit your right on that property, and the sum paid to tie up that property for six months would be gone. Beginning to get the picture?

Let us move on, then, to futures contracts. If you would like to be long a commodity, you can sell a put on that commodity. If you would like to be short a commodity, you can sell a call on that commodity. Options on futures offer the most flexible strategies. There are several reasons for this. First, selling of these instruments does not require the same onerous margin requirements as in the equities markets. Second, they are vastly more flexible in their very nature. These instruments lend themselves to complicated strategies far more readily than do the options on equities. As we get further into the discussion of options in Part II, you will begin to see this flexibility.

LEARNING THE REST OF THE LINGO

Now that you know the significance of puts and calls, it is appropriate to introduce the working jargon of the industry. These will help you become more option savvy.

Underlying Instrument

The term *underlying* refers to the security, the instrument responsible for options pricing. Notice, nowhere did I indicate whether it is a put or a call. *Underlying* essentially describes a stock, bond, commodity, or currency on which a reference option is based. If I am talking about selling a covered call on my IBM stock, I am talking about the underlying instrument (i.e., IBM), not the call, not the put, not General Motors, or any other instrument. An option is a derivative and as such is based on the price of something else.

Exercise Price

The *exercise price* or *strike price* is a price at which the underlying security will be either called away or put to you in the event that the underlying security achieves the price of the option. For example, if the exercise price for the IBM option is 85, that then is the exercise price or the strike price of that particular option. If IBM is trading at 85, it is trading at the strike price. There are many strike prices available for each underlying instrument; some have more, as in the indexes like the S&P 500 or the Russell 1000, and some have less, like GE.

Expiration

Each option sold has an expiration date—a date in the future when this contract will expire. For example, suppose you owned a call option on IBM with a strike price of 90 for March 2006, due to expire on March 17, 2006, and that the stock closed the session at 83 on that Friday. On Monday, March 20, if the stock opens at 95, you have no claim to that stock. It doesn't matter to you because your option to buy expired on Friday and settled on Saturday, and you have no further rights with regard to that option. If you wanted to have your option exercised (exercise your rights), you would have had to let your brokerage house know that; further, you would have had to have done so on March 17, 2006, before the close. You had a right to exercise, but it expired before the rally in the stock.

Assigned Option

The term *assigned* is generally used in options trading when referring to an option that you sold. The buyer exercises his rights and you are assigned the position.

Abandoned Option

There is yet another term used with respect to the actions regarding an option; that term is *abandoned*. It is the buyer's right or privilege to abandon his option. Why would he do that? Perhaps he doesn't want to either buy or sell the stock. This usually occurs when the underlying closes at expiration at or within a few cents of the strike price or is at-the-money (on the target price).

Expire Worthless

Three new words in our options vocabulary—exercise, assign, and abandon—all describe the probable actions that will be taken at expiration. *Expire worthless* means that, at expiration, there is absolutely *no* value left in that option, not a penny. The earlier IBM example was of an out-of-the-money option, or an option that was not at the strike price of the underlying. Out-of-the-money options indicate that your price is away from the market. In the IBM example, you owned a 90 call and that the stock was trading at 83; you own an out-of-the-money option. If you had sold that option, you would have sold an out of the money option. Now, say that was a put; that would change the classification to in-the-money. If you owned a 90 put on IBM and the stock was trading at 83, it would be 7 points in-the-money; 90 minus 83 equals 7; that is the intrinsic value of that option. If you sold the 90 put, it would be the same 7 points in-the-money; this is its intrinsic value. But remember when you sell a put you are agreeing to buy the underlying at that price. Thus, the holder of that put is making money because you have agreed to buy the underlying for 90. That is an example of an in-the-money put.

Time Value

If you sell or buy an out-of-the-money option, it has no intrinsic value; to understand the value you must calculate the *time value*, or time premium of that option. That is calculated by taking the strike price and removing the actual current price of the underlying. Again, go back to the IBM example; remember the option is for 90 and we are now talking about a call. The stock is at 83. The difference between 90 and 83 is the time value or premium.

Premium

If you are a seller of an option, you will receive payment for taking that risk. This payment is called the *premium*. Back to the IBM example. Say you sold a call option with a strike price of 100 for January 2007 and you received 1.05 per share. The money that you received is called the premium. Each option sold represents 100 shares thus you received $105 for every option sold. I hope you are beginning to see that options can increase your return. We just learned the difference between 100 and 83 (17 points) is how far out-of-the-money the option is. The premium of 1.05 a share is also the time value, or time premium, of that option as well as a calculation for the volatility of that option. Why? Because that option has no intrinsic value.

Volatility

It is clear that somebody believes that IBM will be at 100 by January of 2007; otherwise, why would they pay 1.05 for that option? Did they just pick that number out of thin air, or was there a method used to arrive at this number? Yes, there is a method used to arrive at this value, part of which is dependent on the volatility of the underlying issue. So what is *volatility*? It is a measure of how much this underlying tends to move. For example, say IBM moves between 100 and 90 in a year. That volatility is based on either historic or implied volatility. Historic volatility is that volatility seen in the stock when looking back into history. This volatility can be for the stock as well as the option. They have different volatilities but their volatilities are linked. Why linked? Because the option is a derivative of the underlying or the stock. Derivative because it is dependent on the price behavior of the stock to give it a value.

Implied volatility is the market's perception of the future movement of the subject. We find this by using the current option prices and the Black-Scholes option pricing model. We use historic volatility to judge our current implied volatility to help us understand whether we are in a high-, average-, or low-volatility environment. Implied volatility explains the current price of the option. When we look back at its history we discover which environment we are residing in—one of high, average, or low volatility. This is important because, as option sellers, we would love to have a high implied volatility. As option buyers, we want a low volatility when compared to historic volatility.

Did you ever wonder why, just after you have bought or sold a call, the market rises, but that call does not rise? Or perhaps you have been short a call in a falling market and that call did not fall. Well, all of these seemingly weird occurrences are the result of a change in volatility, which usually accompanies the declines in the market.

As an example, say, you sell a call on the S&P 500. The market declines and that call's value rises; it is carried at an increased value in your account. At this point, you are probably scratching your head and saying "What the—." You did not consider that at the same time the market was dropping and the call was rising, the VIX, a measure of volatility calculated based on the at-the-money and out-of-the-money options in the two forward months of the S&P 500, rose from 18 to 21 and then up to 23. What does this have to do with the price of the call? Well, quite a bit! As the VIX rises, you can see fear entering the trade. That fear initiates a ballooning in the premiums as the probability of a greater move is priced into the trade. There is also a fear that the market will no longer be predictable and probably will trade in a wider range, increasing the probability of the trade going south or north. All of this fear and uncertainty is priced into the value of the option. Thus in a declining market the value of a call might actually rise rather than fall, even though the market is moving in the opposite direction.

There is another attribute that is very interesting about options. Have you noticed that the deep-in-the-money options reflect the value of the stock, plus the time to expiration, the volatility change, and the probability of such an occurrence, whereas options that are less in-the-money reflect only some small extra value. Thus, a deep-in-the-money call on the Russell 1000, say a 630 call for August, is priced at 50.30, while a 660 call for August has a value of 28.60. The futures are at 670. Now, 630 plus 50.30 gives you a futures price of 680.30, while 660 plus 28.6 gives you a price of 686.60. Why the difference? The 690 calls for August are trading at 11.50, which would project a value of 701.50. As you go deeper in-the-money, a lot of the risk is removed; thus, you aren't going to be paid for taking that risk. As the risk increases, the premium for assuming that risk is reflected in the price of the option. This works for puts as well as calls.

The day these quotes were based on, the VIX or volatility index was trading between 21 and 23; that was its trading range for the day. These are real numbers. When the VIX was trading between 21 and 23, the options were priced at:

August 640 calls closed the session at 45.50.

August 672 calls closed the session at 23.30.

August 690 calls closed the session at 13.50.

The September futures contract closed the session at 675.

Today, the VIX dropped 25.91 percent, closing at 15.90. The VIX opened the session at 21.05; so, how does this drop in volatility affect the price of the options? Here is a quote of the options one day later, after a major 15-point 2.22 percent rally in the Russell 1000:

August 640 calls closed at 56.15.

August 672 calls closed at 30.90.

August 690 calls closed at 18.50.

The September futures contract closed the session at 690.

Wouldn't it seem logical that the 640 calls should close at 60.50? And the 672 calls close at 38.80? Instead, the volatility was reduced, causing the options to not appreciate as much as would have been expected. How did that happen? Well, some of the fear was removed.

Here we are, just one week after the trade was put on, and the VIX has collapsed to 15.52. The September Russell 1000 futures contract is trading at 687. What do you suppose happened to those options in one week?

August 640 calls closed at 51.75.

August 672 calls closed at 25.50.

August 690 calls closed at 13.25.

The September futures contract closed the session at 687.

Notice that the August 640 calls are 4.40 lower, with the futures trading 3 points lower. This is a deep in-the-money call, so you would expect it to track the future, but what you also see is time erosion and volatility implosion.

The 672 calls are now 5.40 lower than they were with the futures losing 3 points. The 690 calls took a 5.25 haircut on the 3-point drop in the VIX. What we are seeing is the effect that a week of time and a decrease in volatility can have on the pricing of the options. At this time, I have to remind you that the VIX, as a measurement of volatility, dropped merely from 15.90 to 15.52; that is not a huge drop.

Just to amplify the effect that a change in volatility will have on options pricing, look back at the prices of the options with the futures at 675. The 640 calls were priced at 45.50, whereas now, a week later and after a

25 percent drop in volatility as measured by the VIX, the calls are priced at 51.75. The difference in the price of the call is 6.25, while the difference in the futures is 12 points. Get the picture?

Here we are one day later with the VIX up a mere 0.36 on the day and the Russell 1000 September futures contract down 3.50 on the day. Let's look at the options:

> August 640 calls closed the session at 48.55, down 3.20 on the day, a 6.18 percent drop.
>
> August 672 calls closed the session at 22.85, down 2.65 on the day, a 10.39 percent drop.
>
> August 690 calls closed the session at 11.20, down 2.05 on the day, a 15.47 percent drop.

What becomes very clear when looking at these numbers from day to day is that the deeper in-the-money the calls are, the less percentage drop will be seen if the market retreats. However, a call that is out-of-the-money or near-the-money will have a greater percentage move on that same retreat of the market. Now, it is true that every day is an erosion day. In other words, these options waste away approaching expiration. The options that we are looking at are two months away from expiration; those that are closer to expiration are having a more dramatic reaction to the advancing of time.

Theoretical Value

Theoretical value of the option includes a probability calculation, risk-free rates, and time. This is the famous Black-Scholes option pricing formula. Theoretical value involves probability of the expected return. When you use money, you must factor in costs, such as carrying costs, as well as dividends; these also contribute to the expected return for the investment. The option trader is always looking for a theoretical edge at which to buy undervalued options and to sell overvalued options, capturing the mispriced leg as profit. The goal is to sell the overpriced option and to buy the underpriced option: an option trader's dream!

Naked Call

Naked calls are where you don't own the stock, commodity, bond, or instrument on which the call is being written or sold. Therefore, you are naked. Should the issue be called from you and exercised, you will have to go to the market, buy the issue, and then deliver it to the holder of that option. There is unlimited risk on the upside should this issue take off. This is considered to be a risky strategy; however, I will show you how to fix that in Part Three as we talk about different strategies using options in up markets, trading range markets, and declining markets. Many times, as futures traders, we sell options without owning the underlying contracts. In equities, a good way to buy a stock that you absolutely would like to own is by selling a naked put. By doing so, you are agreeing to purchase that stock at a given price and by a certain date if assigned. The purchaser of the right to sell you that stock pays you money, the premium. Whether you will own the stock in the future or not, you get to keep that money. The purchaser has bought some insurance on his stock that assures him that he can sell that stock at a given price for a period certain. If you were to sell a naked call, you would not own the underlying instrument. You would be obligated to deliver that instrument should the assignment be made, at which point you would have two choices: one, to buy the stock and deliver it, or, two, to remain short the stock and deliver borrowed stock to the clearinghouse.

Covered Call

You own the issue on which the *covered call* is being written. Your risk is limited to the strike price on the upside and zero unless the stock declines. There is always a risk on the downside. This is a very conservative method of increasing your yield on your securities. This is allowed in pension funds, individual retirement accounts (IRAs), and other retirement vehicles.

Naked Put

In a *naked put,* your risk is defined by the strike price of the put. You are agreeing to buy the issue at that price; therefore your risk is limited.

Covered Put

Covered puts are risky. In this position, you are short the instrument and sell the put option. Why is it risky? Because, by selling the put option, you are agreeing to buy the instrument on which it is written. Thus, if you are agreeing to buy the instrument and you are short the instrument, this action makes you a little long. The risk is that you have no coverage on the upside and, should the instrument rally further, you have unlimited risk as the price rises.

USING OPTIONS AND WHY THEY CAN BE FUN

Options can be used in many ways, but for now let's consider the use of options as a hedge and a speculation. Obviously, speculation brings to mind gambling, and in fact this action can be similar. By buying an option, the buyer is gambling on the movement of the underlying instrument. Why not just buy or sell the instrument? That is a good question, one that can be answered by one word: leverage!

When purchasing options, you are trying to maximize your possible outcomes with the least amount of money. If you believe that IBM is going to go to $200 per share (suppose it is now trading at $83.30), you may decide to buy an option on IBM with a strike price of $130 that expires in January 2008. This call will cost you 55 cents per share, or $55 for every 100 shares of IBM. Again, this is a gamble; you are wagering that IBM will be at $130 a share or above by the third Friday in January of 2008. For that privilege, you are paying $55 per 100-share lot, or $55 per call. Should IBM close that session on the third Friday in January 2008 at $200 per share, you are a huge winner. Should IBM close the session on the third Friday in January 2008 at $129, you lost $55; end of report.

As a hedge, if you are short the instrument you might want to buy the call to define your risk. Again, say you are short IBM and you want to limit your upside risk exposure on that stock. You might buy the IBM call, which would put a ceiling on the risk you are willing to take with that short position. Short IBM at 83.30, long a 100 call; your risk is limited by that call, but only to the time of expiration and not a second longer.

Why buy a call? Well, if the stock goes up wildly, you have a very small investment relative to the cost of the underlying, with almost unlimited upside. Should the stock go down, you have spent only the premium paid for that option without receiving a benefit other than insurance. Suppose instead you bought IBM stock and the stock dropped 10 points; 10 times 100 is equal to a loss of $1,000 for 100 shares of IBM.

Now, say you bought the call and paid $200 for that call. Your cost is $200, not $1,000 per 100 shares. Beginning to get the idea?

As a call writer, you are limiting your upside on that stock or instrument, but that sale increases your returns on the underlying. Should the stock drop, you have the loss on the stock to deal with and the option premium helps deflect some of the costs of the underlying's fall.

Say you bought a put and the stock drops like a rock. You are in a position to take a large profit, with a limited cost base and a limited risk. Say you own the stock on which you bought the put. Here, you have bought an insurance type product that will protect you on the downside, but for a limited time only (expiration date of the option). Should the underlying rally, you receive no gain from the money used in purchasing the put.

As a put writer (seller), should the stock rally, you can only make the premium paid to you for writing that put. Should the stock or the underlying security tank, you are long and wrong—but you can only go to zero!

COMBINING OPTIONS PURCHASES

Combining options purchases and sales helps you achieve a goal, whether it be taking advantage of a possible move up, a down move, or just inefficiencies in the market.

Conversions or Collars

This is a really neat way of locking up the return on a stock, futures contract, or underlying security. In this operation, there are three trades involved. First, you are long the underlying; second, you sell the call (a covered write); and third, you buy a protective put. Here is how this works:

Say you continue to like IBM and you have purchased the stock for $83 per share. You bought 100 shares at $8,300, plus commission, which, if you go to a deep discount broker, could be as low as $5 to $7 per transaction. The stock pays a dividend four times per year, in March, June, September, and December, and you want to capture that; the yield on IBM is 80 cents per share or 0.997 percent. If you want to capture that dividend, you must be sure to sell an option that will expire after the stock goes ex-dividend (i.e., trades without its dividend).

It is now March, and you sold the April 85 call for 1.20 and bought the April 80 put for 0.50. You have basically protected your stock, putting a cap on any possible loss at $80 per share. However, you also have capped the possible gains you can make on the security at $85 per share; but you also will get the dividend, which is 80 cents divided by four (pays quarterly). Now, if you move the position to May, you could get 1.70 for the call, but would have to pay 90 cents for the put. See Table 7.3 for an illustration of this example.

In both cases, you have placed limits on the possible loss you will tolerate and capped the profit you can make on the transaction. In both cases, you will be paid the dividend and will have limited your downside risk; of course, you're giving up some of the upside, but this return is better than you would have just sitting there waiting for the stock to pay a dividend. There is yet one more possibility: that the stock closes on expiration between 80 and 85, which would give you the opportunity to do this again.

TABLE 7.3   IBM Options Example

April		May	
Buy shares at	83.00	Buy shares at	83.00
Receive from call	1.20	Receive from call	1.70
Pay for put	0.50	Pay for put	0.90
Get dividend	0.20	Get dividend	0.20
Cost basis	82.10	Cost basis	82.00
Maximum loss on trade	2.10	Maximum loss	2.00
Maximum gain	2.90	Maximum gain	3.00
Holding time	1 month	Holding time	2 months

True, you could have bought a put at-the-money, which would have had more protection for the downside but would have returned less and actually would have cost money. Sometimes these collars are put on to close the position immediately after the dividend payment.

Straddles

A straddle is buying an at-the-money call and an at-the-money put. Why do this? Well, if the underlying has a violent move in either direction, you can be a big winner. Remember, only one side of this will pay off. This is acknowledging that you don't know where the market is going to go, but you do believe that this is going to be a big move; so you will gamble on both, knowing that half of the position might yet have to be discarded as worthless. When would you use this? If Google, for example, is coming out with an earnings report and you believe that it is going to make a difference in the price of the stock, you might want to buy both the put and the call. Say Google came out with great earnings numbers and the stock rallied; you would make money on the call but the put would be worthless. If the opposite is true, you would make money on the put and the call would be worthless. You are straddling the market, standing on both sides and declaring that there will be a huge move, but not making a prediction as to its direction.

EUROPEAN VERSUS AMERICAN OPTIONS

This difference between European and American options is really trivial, but must be stated. European options can be exercised only on the last day prior to expiration. American options can be exercised at any time up to and including the expiration date. Why is that important? Because there may come a time when the purchaser of an option wants to exercise that right early—perhaps as a result of a buyout, merger, trade, or margin relief. Margin relief is generally seen with puts. The buyer of the put has bought insurance against the price loss in her stock. If the stock plummets and she has been holding this stock in her margin account she is paying margin interest and may want to be relieved of this cost by selling her stock early to the seller of the put. Remember, if you sold the put, you are obligated to do something. In this case, it is to buy the stock.

Let us again use the Home Depot example. You sold the put for January 2007 and received $115 for doing so. Great! Here we are in October and the stock is trading at $35. The person who bought that put from you now wants to unload the stock, so he exercises that put purchase and you own Home Depot at $37.50 per share. This is an example of an American style option assignment.

Now let's look at a European style option. You sold a put on XYZ Company for the March 2007 expiration with a strike price of 40. It is January and the stock is selling for $20 per share. It won't be put to you because it isn't puttable until the expiration. By expiration, the stock is back to $40 and the stock was not put to you. The premium is the cost of the option.

What, then, is a put and how can it be used as an investment aid? Again, if you purchase a put, you own a right, which you may or may not wish to use. However, if you sell a put, you are obliged to do something in the future and that something is to purchase that stock at a given price by the end of a given time, our date certain. Say you sold a January put on your favorite stock; you are contractually obliged to buy that stock at the strike price by the January expiration date. Say the stock is trading much higher than the put strike price by January; obviously, you won't be given the opportunity to buy the stock at that strike price; however, if the stock is trading below the put strike price, well, the stock will be put to you.

Suppose you sell a November 40 put on Home Depot. You would get paid 1.40 per share or $140: 1.40 times 100 equals $140 for 100 shares.

You would do this only if you wanted to buy Home Depot stock, because you are on the hook, so to speak, to buy the stock at $40 a share, and even if the stock is somewhere below that level you will be the proud owner of the shares at $40 each. You will have to put good faith margin in your account until this option expires because of the agreement to purchase the shares. The brokerage house needs to have that money available to pay for that stock in the event of a put being exercised against you. You will not be charged margin interest because you haven't bought the stock as yet; the money is a promise to pay, a sort of deposit on the transaction. As noted earlier, you will be paid for agreeing to purchase the stock and this payment will be made immediately. If at any time until the expiration date the holder of the option wants to sell his stock to you, you have agreed to buy it at $40 per share. Now, if you sold one put, you have agreed to buy 100 shares at $40 each for a total cost of $4,000, plus commissions. Your margin requirement was initially $2,000, which could have been in the form of stocks, bonds, or any marginable credit in your account. Yes, you could use the $140 you were paid in premium to reduce that margin amount.

If you had been the purchaser of the put option, you purchased the right to sell your stock at $40 per share. As a holder of the shares, you bought some short-term insurance on your stock. Should the stock plunge to $20 per share before the option expires, it doesn't matter to you because you have the right to sell that stock for $40 per share. These options do expire at a set time in the future, so the buyer of the put has protection only for that time; then he must sell another put.

Many investors like to sell puts because they receive the payment from the premium, and they well might like to buy that stock at that price. It is conceivable that you could continue selling puts on your favorite stocks without becoming the owner of the shares, just as it is possible that you can sell calls on your securities and not sell the securities.

CONCLUSION

This chapter has presented the most basic information about options. If you understand what you've read here, nothing in options will be hard to comprehend. The beauty of options is that they are somewhat abstract and, as such, you can use your imagination to construct and build positions. Options strategy is rather like war games or chess; you must plot and analyze the positions and estimate the likely reaction to such positions.

When I was a rookie broker in 1981 at Thomson McKinnon Securities (a firm that is no longer in existence, having been gobbled up by Prudential and eventually eaten by a larger fish called Wachovia), I was forever trying to learn new ways of making money. I clearly remember interest rates in the high teens and the prime rate over 20 percent. It was really hard to explain to clients why they should invest in the stock market when they were earning 18 and 19 percent almost risk free in the money markets. As a baby broker, my education was a self-study course and the Series 7 exam. Once I passed, on St. Patrick's Day, I was given a desk and a phone and told to go to work. Great. Doing what? The manager said, "Sell stock!" I asked, "What stock?" and he replied, "Read the research reports and pick one. There is the phone—go for it!" I soon developed a phone phobia, a typical result of constantly being rejected by the recipients of the cold calls. Faced with both the hostile investor and a high money market rate, I had to solve this problem or lose my job.

In that moment of frustration and stupidity, an idea was born: Marry the high interest rates with options. So started this imaginative journey into options, using convertible bonds for the yield and selling calls to improve the return, in order to beat the extremely high interest paid by the money markets. Remember, too, that the market was tanking daily and I had to find a sort of safe investment. You probably are wondering how I was able to write a covered call on a convertible bond. Convertible bonds are hybrid securities, part bond and part security (as discussed in Chapter 6). They are a bond with a call on a stock united in a single issue. Convertible bonds convert into a set number of shares and at a fixed price; therefore, it is possible to view this security as part equity, and because of that, you can sell a call on that stock. Because it is part equity, it satisfies the requirement of owning the security to sell a covered call. Without the convertible bond, the call would be naked and there would be a considerable margin requirement. Also, it would not qualify to be held in a retirement account, but by using the convertible bond, you overcome that problem.

It is this sort of imaginative trading that can help you make money and increase the returns on your investments. Most good ideas are born of necessity. Some of my best trades have been as a result of an error. Today, more than ever before, a working knowledge of options is necessary to insulate the investment you make as well as to maximize your returns on your investments. Remember, you can own a stock and just get the 1.2 percent dividend yield, or you can enhance that yield by selling covered calls on that stock. It is up to you: Do you want to watch others make money, or do you want to be the one making the money?

CHAPTER 8

Using Options in Trending Markets

This chapter shows you the best ways to take advantage of a trending market. Markets that trend enjoy more predictable movement than do markets that don't trend. Also, in trending markets, options become pricier. This can be both advantageous and penalizing. Professional options traders do not try to take advantage of trending markets; rather, they try to take advantage of mispriced options. These are options that are just slightly off-kilter, and either are priced less than you can sell them for or are worth more than they would cost you. This miswriting is an options trader's bread and butter. However, options pros don't care whether the market goes up or down; the entire purpose of their trading is to capture this mispriced advantage and to hedge away any risk of the position. This means that when they purchase or sell an option, they may continue that trade to remove the risk.

Actually, today in the trading ring, there is a trader with about one year of experience in trading, running an options-based hedge fund. He has no formal training in the market but is able to mechanically buy, sell, and hedge a $5 million portfolio without any problems. You may well wonder how he can manage this portfolio. Well, here is the easy answer: If he buys an option, he looks to his computer to see how many futures contracts he must buy or sell. He also can figure out that if he were to buy in New York he might be able to sell in Chicago, keeping the portfolio delta neutral. It is a mechanical trade done without an opinion. He is better than most traders who have an opinion because he just does the trade without thinking about where the market is going or what it might do in the future. To him, it is irrelevant and unnecessary information.

REMOVING THE RISK FROM THE TRADE

Removing the risk sounds easy, but in reality it isn't. However, you don't have to be a math genius; a good computer program or even a calculator should be adequate to serve your most exotic requirements. Here is the idea: By selling or buying options you might be able to remove the risk of the trade, much as was shown possible in a collar or conversion in the preceding chapter. How do we do that? Well, now we have to enter the world of the Greeks to try to explain the protocol.

Delta

The first word (or letter) that is of great importance is *delta*. When relating to an option, delta describes the probability of achieving the price.

Delta also can be defined as the numerical amount of stocks or other issues needed to satisfy the probable future need to keep this position neutral. If you have a delta of 0.50 you are long half a contract or 50 shares of stock and you know that you are long; therefore, to neutralize the position, you need to sell half a contract or 50 shares of the underlying. This is how delta is used; it is not just a recommendation to do so. Delta is a positive number for a long; it is a negative number for a short position. Therefore, if you sell a put with a negative delta of 0.50 and sell a call with a positive delta of 0.50, you are neutral. You want to know why? Okay, selling a put makes you long; selling a call makes you short; therefore, you are long 0.50 and short 0.50. Your position is neutral for the moment. Yes, this changes all the time and it has to be adjusted.

Delta also describes the movement that the option will make per one point in the underlying. For example: A stock moves one point. The underlying option you own has a 0.50 delta; therefore, it will move 50 cents per $1 move in the stock. If it has a 1.00 delta, it will move dollar for dollar with the stock. This number changes, which will lead us to another ancient Greek term: gamma (described in the next section).

Positive deltas can be achieved by going long calls or by buying stock or the underlying security or commodity. You can have a positive delta if you sell a put. This would make you long at a given price in a time certain, but the action would cause you to have a long position. Buying any security (even commodities) on which the options are being priced will cause a positive delta.

Negative deltas can be achieved by selling short a security, selling a call, buying a put, or selling the underlying. Going short, even synthetically, is a negative delta action. Let us think about a line on the page like this:

Negative ---------------Zero ----------------Positive

Short --------------------Flat ----------------------Long

Long puts ---------------Flat -------------- Short puts

Short calls --------------Flat ---------------Long calls

Additionally, as you approach expiration, you will note that the deep-in-the-money options will act very much like the underlying. They do not necessarily track the underlying when there is a great deal of time left—even an in-the-money option will not have a delta of 1.00, because there is the probability and possibility of the market moving it the wrong way. As you approach expiration, that window of opportunity closes and the delta moves higher.

In options circles, much talk revolves around volatility. When the volatility is low, the traders will generally buy options. As the volatility increases, options are sold.

Gamma

Should you want to calculate the rate of change of the delta of the option, you look to the *gamma* for that information. It can also be described as the curvature of that option as it approaches maturity. This Greek tells you how much the delta will change per move in the underlying. Does the delta go up when the stock's price goes up? Yes, this measurement will tell you how much that change would be. Gammas are always positive numbers.

Understandably, the gamma for an in- or at-the-money option will be greater than for an out-of-the-money option. Let us work through this one. Say you own a call option with a strike of 50, expiring in several weeks. The stock is at 60; therefore, your option is in-the-money by 10 points. It stands to reason that as the price of the stock moves your option will move in lockstep with the stock. The amount of the movement, per point in the stock, is reflected in the gamma, which tells you how much the delta will be moved by this stock's movements.

Theta

Theta is the time decay of an option, or the erosion factor. This number is a negative number because it describes the loss from option time decay.

The decay is not uniform and accelerates as the option enters the month of its expiration.

Volatility affects the delta and gamma of an option. You will notice when looking at options chains (the series of options), that chains for volatile issues are higher-priced than are chains of options with low volatility. Many options traders avoid low-volatility stocks, holding that they are poor candidates for an option writing program. Basically, you can't get much for something that doesn't move much. Would you pay money for an option written on a stock that barely moves? Probably not.

Vega

Vega measures the effect that increasing or decreasing volatility will have on an option. Options with high vegas are written on highly volatile issues. This is a mathematical expression, telling us how the option's theoretical value will change due to changes in volatility. The number is based on a 1 percent change in volatility of that issue.

Volatility describes the movements of the issue. Historic volatility describes the issue's past volatility. Current volatility describes how emotional this issue has become describing its movements to the upside and downside. This measurement is important for option traders to take note of. If the vega is 0.30 for every 1 percent move in volatility, the change to the option value will be 0.30.

If you are long futures or the underlying or short, you have no gamma, theta, or vega because you have sold no options. If you are long, your delta will be positive; if you are short, your delta will be negative.

If you bought a call and own no stock or underlying, you have positive delta, positive gamma, negative theta, and positive vega. Why positive delta? Because you are a little long. Positive gamma, because this position will be ruled by your positive delta and your gamma (which is always a positive number), will tell you how much your delta will move with respect to the price of the underlying. Theta will be negative because your option will decay with time. Vega will be positive because this option's price will respond to changes in volatility.

Now let's assume you are short calls naked. You have negative delta because you are short, and negative gamma; time is your friend, so your theta is positive and your vega is negative.

If you are long puts, the delta continues to be negative because you have a synthetic short, your gamma is positive because changes will affect your delta, you have negative theta because time is your enemy (you are long options), and your vega will be positive because changes to volatility will affect your option.

Say you are short puts. Well, that will make you synthetically long (remember you are agreeing to purchase) and your delta will be positive, your gamma will be negative, and your theta positive. While time is usually your friend, vega is negative in this instance.

Rho

Rho is the measurement given to interest rates; if you have positive rho, you want rates to rise; if you have negative rho, you would prefer a contraction of interest rates.

Summary of Greeks

So here it is: If your delta is positive, you would benefit from a rise in the price of the underlying. If your delta is negative, a decline is on your wish list. Positive theta benefits from the erosion of time, because you have sold a wasting asset. If you bought the option, then theta is your enemy and you hope that your option will achieve its goal plus the cost of buying that option by the time the option expires. If you have positive vega, you want volatility to increase; if your vega is negative, you want the underlying to go nowhere. For those who have positive gamma, you want the market to move; for a negative gamma player, you pray for a stagnant market. I didn't mention rho, because it has less value in this current environment options analysis. Today, because interest rates have been stable, rho isn't that important; but when they flip around, that is when this measurement becomes more valuable.

If you are in a trending market, your volatility is fairly reasonable; thus your vega is under control. As to your delta, it will be measurable and your gamma will be fine. We will eliminate the rho, and deal with the theta.

GREEKS FOR GEEKS

If you are long call options in a rising market where the underlying is performing with the market, you have positive delta, your gamma is positive, and your theta is negative. Why? Because every day costs you money on the erosion of value of that option and your vega is positive. Let us go back to the theta, an options seller's old pal and an options buyer's archenemy. We can calculate how much money is lost each day until expiration. As an options buyer, this is a force moving against you. The options market does not move in a straight line; it curves. That curvature can also be described as the gamma. As the option approaches the last month of its life, the curvature increases, reflecting the reduced time available for this option to reach its price goal. The risk in this option position also increases because there is less time for it to achieve the price. Just think about it: If you own an option—for this example, let's use a 90 call on IBM—that will expire in three months, in spite of the stock sitting at the 83 level there is a chance for the stock to achieve 90. Not a great chance, but a chance. As we approach the end of the three months and the stock continues to linger at 83, your chances become more remote that the stock will achieve that price.

By the way, you would expect to see the delta of a deep-in-the-money option register 1.00, but it doesn't. By expiration, it will be approaching the 1.00 level if the option is in-the-money. This happens because the possibility of adverse price moves does not disappear until expiration. I well remember when an overnight bomb threat on options expiration day took a put position that had almost no delta and no bid to a position of value. That option went from zero bid to a bid of 8 overnight, bam! What this is telling you is that the opportunity for an adverse event is there until that puppy expires.

HOW DO YOUR GREEKS ADD UP?

Options sellers enjoy positive theta and negative gamma. Why? Because time is your pal, your best friend. You want negative gamma because you *don't* want price movement, because it will hurt your position. The last thing an option seller wants to see is quick moves on the underlying. As an option buyer, you hate theta and love gamma. Obviously you are happy with price movements and increases in volatility. Even if you are on the wrong side of the fence on this one, the increased volatility will increase the value of your option. You want the vega to increase because the value of the option will increase with the volatility of the underlying.

The market is trending (that means it is going up or going down), but it is doing so in an expected manner. This leaves you with several alternatives. Go with the trend and enjoy the ride. That is, find the securities that are leading the move and jump on the bandwagon. To do this, you will be risking money. Before that action, you have to assess the probability of the move. Our technical analysis knowledge is about to help us make money. We know about puts, calls, and the Greeks. Now we need to get them to work together.

Imagine we are looking at the market and it's in rally mode. Question one will be: Is this the beginning of the trend, or are we coming in at the 11th hour? That is probably one of the most important questions you can ask. It is important in assessing risk and reward—the possibility of a gain in the trade. If you are risking a dollar to make a nickel, don't trade. The risk of losing a dollar is too great against the possible earning of a nickel. However, if you can look at a trade and see that with a dollar of risk you can make at least two or perhaps three dollars, then the trade is worth the risk.

Back to the IBM example, which is trading at 83. Suppose it has been trading between 90 and 78 for the past three months. Technically, the stock is stuck and seems to have trouble getting above 85 and holding there. We also know that the stock seems to bounce off the 79 level, which it has tested at least five times in the past three months. It has a 50-day moving average of 82.05 and a 14-day moving average of 82.62. We also note that the Bollinger bands have become fairly wide and therefore this could be a good time to think about selling options on IBM. Our Bollinger bands are at about 85 for the top one and 82 for the lower one. That should represent 95 percent of the move made in either direction. The indicators are all showing us that there is a liability to the downside. Now, let us look at the possibilities.

If we sell an option, we would like it to be fairly close to expiration so that we can capture the premium and close out the trade without waiting a long time. We check the options chain to review which options look inviting to sell. April has three weeks left and most of the juice is gone from those options, so how about May, which will give us about seven weeks for the trade? April 85 calls are selling for 1.00 and the 80 puts are selling for 0.45. If we up the ante, we could get 2.25 for the April 85 puts. Okay, so now let us look into the May options.

The May options for the same strikes are as follows: The 85 call for May is 1.40 and the 80 put for May is 0.80. Okay, say we sold the May 85 call and bought the May 80 put; we would collect 60 cents and have unlimited risk on the upside. Is that trade worth it? Short and long answer on that one is no. We could make almost the same money on the April trade; remember, get a dollar and pay 45 cents; that is 55 cents with three weeks to go, rather than the seven or so weeks on the May expiration. We could sell the put for 45 cents, sell the call for a buck, and buy the 90 call to keep our risk to a minimum on the upside. The 90 call will cost us 15 cents. (See Table 8.1.) This interesting trade is a call spread with a short put. Basically,

TABLE 8.1 IBM Strangle with a Twist

Action	Premium Received/ Paid
Sell April 85 call	$1.00
Sell April 80 put	$0.45
Buy April 90 call	$0.15
Total proceeds	$1.30

TABLE 8.2 IBM Trade with Addition of the Lower Put

Action	Premium Received/ Paid
Sell IBM 85 call	$1.00
Buy IBM 90 call	$0.15
Sell IBM 80 put	$0.45
Buy IBM 75 put	$0.10
Short one call spread	$0.85 credit
Short one put spread	$0.35 credit
Total proceeds collected	$1.20

it makes you long IBM at 80 and also sells IBM at 85; but in case the stock rallies, you have a long call and the right to buy the stock at 90. Of course, if the stock falls to 77, you might have paid 80 for it and have an immediate loss of three bucks; but you did collect money to do this trade and there is nothing stopping you from selling a call again on this stock.

We still have risk on the downside, so we can buy the 75 put for a cost of 0.10, which would bring our proceeds down to 1.20 in the kitty (see Table 8.2).

What is our risk? Good question. Should IBM go to 88 bucks, we lose 3.00; should IBM go to 89, we lose 4.00; should IBM go to 90, we lose 5.00. So we are collecting 1.20 with the possible loss of 5.00. Is that trade probable? No, but it is possible. On the downside: Since we sold the 80 put, we are now long at 80, but we have that loss locked to the same five bucks. The maximum loss on that trade is 5.00 minus 1.20 (the option premium received), considering we might hold that position to expiration. This is not a delta neutral trade; the trade is slightly short. The deltas are as follows: On the 85 call the delta is .366, on the 90 call it is .077, on the 75 put it is –0.0211, and on the 80 put is –0.20. Our short call spread has a delta of .28 and our short put spread has a delta of –0.1789. To correct for this, we should sell another 80 put and get the extra 45 cents in premium. Then the position will be neutral.

RATIO SPREADS

What we have done is balanced our short calls with short puts. This means that we are short the stock if it trades above 85 and long the stock if it trades below 80, but we have collars on so that we have limited any loss that might occur as a consequence of this trade. As a matter of fact, we have calculated what our maximum gain can be as well as our maximum loss. This isn't a great trade, but it is a good example of how options can be used in combinations. In this example, we are using a call spread and a ratio put spread.

Spreads can be defined as the taking of a position on one side of the trade and offsetting it by the other side of the trade. In our example, we sold the 85 call for more than we paid to buy the 90 call; thus we were short the spread: short the 85 and long the 90. Had we reversed the position, we would have been long the call spread: long the 85 and short the 90. We would have been the buyer of the spread. As a seller of the spread, we sold the 85 and bought the 90. Another way of stating this is:

One is a *credit spread*; you get paid.

The other is a *debit spread*; it costs you money.

The same is true of the put spreads. We sold the put spread. Remember, we sold the 80 for more than it cost us to buy the 75; therefore, we were paid; thus it was a credit spread. Had we done the reverse, it would have been a debit spread; we would have been a buyer and it would have cost us money.

This type of credit or debit spread works well in trending markets because you are hedging your gamble. In a market that is in rally mode, you might buy the spread, gambling that the market will continue to rise, but hedging the bet by selling a call against the call you are long. In a downtrending market, you might buy a put spread, which would be another debit spread. You are buying the higher strike and selling a lower strike to reduce your cost basis. By the way, when you do that, you also reduce your profit potential by defining the maximum you can make on the trade.

CONCLUSION

So far, this book has gone to great lengths to help you identify trends—is the market going up, down, or sideways? If it is indeed going sideways, the volatility will be drying up and you won't get enough for that option to really make you happy. It is your job to decide what the direction of the issue is. Once that has been done, you must look at support and resistance. Now you are armed and ready to fight in the options arena. If you have discovered that the stock price is relatively high and that it always has trouble at these levels, why not sell a call on that stock? If the stock is really cheap and you would like to own it, why not sell a put on that stock?

CHAPTER 9

Using Options in Trading Range Markets

T rading in range-bound markets can cause great mental stress for options buyers, because the market seems to be stuck, unable to break either to the upside or to the downside. However, these markets that are stuck in a range can be one of the options seller's best friends. Why? Because you, as an option seller, can identify a range and then use it to enhance your option position. These ranges, if they last a long time, can, however, lead to complacency. We have also learned that the longer a market remains in a trading range, the larger the move will likely be when it is finally seen.

This chapter shows you some ways to cash in on issues that seem to be stuck in a range. It covers several strategies, including butterflies, condors, trees, and packages, that work well in this sort of a market.

BUTTERFLIES

An option butterfly is a combination of three option positions, which when combined resemble a butterfly on the chart. It is obtained when one is long two options or short two options, both at the same price, and at the same time an option above the two options is sold or bought and an option below the two options is sold or bought. Should you be long the middle two options and short the wings, you are said to be "long the butterfly." If you are short the middle two options and long the wings, you are "short the butterfly." This option strategy works well in a trading range market.

Butterfly.

Long Butterfly

Let us examine a long butterfly strategy. We believe that stock XYZ is stuck in a trading range and we see nothing that makes us believe that this range will be breached. We have identified both the top of the range and the bottom of the range. Now, we buy options around the price of the stock. Say the stock is trading at 73 and has a trading range of 69 to 81. We

TABLE 9.1 XYZ What-ifs: Long Butterfly

Action	Premium Received/ Paid
Sell 70 call	$500
Buy 2 75 calls @ $200	$400
Sell 80 call	$ 70
Total proceeds on trade	$570
Total cost for trade	$400
Net proceeds	$170

have identified the range and we are ready to look at our butterfly. We would buy two calls with a strike price of 75 and sell one call with a strike price of 80 and one call with a strike price of 70. What happens if the stock goes to 81? You are long two calls that have a value of 10, a call on which you are short with a value of 1, and a call on which you are short with a value of zero (0).

Let's try using dollar amounts. Say we paid $2.00 for the 75 call; remember that we bought two of these calls, so our cost would be $4.00. Further, remember that $2.00 actually means $200; thus, we have spent $400 on this part of the trade. We sold the 80 call and have received $0.70, so there is a $70 credit in our account. We also sold a deep-in-the-money 70 call for $5.00, which translates into a credit of $500. We have spent $400 and have taken in $570. Should the market remain in the trading range we have identified, we will walk away from the trade with a profit. (See Table 9.1.)

So, let us run the various different scenarios. (See Table 9.2.) At 81, both of our short calls are in-the-money. Now, this illustrates the beginning of our problem. We are long the 75, but short two in-the-money calls. The 70 short call is covered by one of the 75 long calls, so that one is no longer of concern. But we are short the 80 call. Not to worry; that call is covered by the other 75 long call. We will lose on the trade, but not all that much.

At 81, what is the package worth? The 70 short call is worth $11.00 or $1,100; the 75 long calls are worth $6.00 each, which is a total of $1,200; the 80 short call is worth $1.00 or $100. The trade is worth zero, but the costs will be a negative on our profit and loss statement.

What happens to this trade if the market closes at, say, 77? The 80 short call is worth zero; the 75 long calls are worth $2.00 each or $400; the 70 short call is worth $7.00 or $700. These proceeds total negative

TABLE 9.2 Long Butterfly Scenarios

XYZ 81 at Expiration

Sold 1 70 call	Received 5	Now debit of 11	
Bought 2 75 calls	Paid 2 each	Now worth 10	
Sold 1 80 call	Received .70	Now debit of 1	
	Total proceeds 1.70	Total debit 2.00	
Trade	Received 1.70	Total loss .30	

What if: XYZ 90 at Expiration

Sold 1 70 call	Received t	Now debit of 20	−20
Bought 2 75 calls	Paid 2 each = 4	Credit of 30	+30
Sold 1 80 call	Received .70	Debit of 10	−10
Trade	Received 1.70	Zero	Zero

What if: XYZ at 79 on Expiration

Sold 1 70 call	Received 5	Debit 9	− 9
Bought 2 75 calls	Paid 2 each = 4	Credit 8	+ 8
Sold 1 80 call	Received .70	Zero	0
Trade	Received 1.70	Debit 1.00	.70

$300. But not so fast; remember we took in $570; so we actually have a profit of $270.

Cost	$400
Proceeds	$570
At Expiration:	
Receipt	$400
Debit	$700
Total	$300
Original Proceeds $570 − $300 = $270	

Here is an example with IBM. IBM is trading at 83.30. The July 85 calls are trading at $2.45. The July 90 calls are trading at $0.85, and the July 80 calls are trading at $5.50. What do we have now? We will purchase two July 85 calls for a cost of $2.45 each or $490. We will sell one July 90 call and receive $85. We will sell one July 80 call and receive $550.

Proceeds on trade	$635
Total cost for trades	$490
Net proceeds	$145

Should IBM close at 85, our two long options will be worth zero, but our short 90 call will be also worth zero. The 80 call will be worth $500. We collected $635 when we put this trade on; therefore we have a gain of $135. Say the stock closes at 79. The calls are all worthless and we have collected $635. You might well ask: What is the most we can make on that trade? Should the stock close at 90 on expiration, that would be our maximum gain. The 80 call would be worth $1,000, the two 85 calls would be worth $1,000, and the 90 call would be worth zero. Again, we would have made $635 on that trade. At no time did we buy any stock. This is a trade done without a stock purchase.

Now, let us do it with futures!

We randomly picked July coffee as our objective. Coffee is currently trading are 109.85 for the July expiry. The butterfly will be based on the July options expiration. Each point in coffee is worth $375.

Buy two July 110 calls at a cost of 6.57 each = 13.14 $4,927.50
Sell one July 100 call for 12.06 $4,522.50
Sell one July 120 call for 3.40 $1,275.00
Cost $4,927.50
Proceeds $5,797.50
We collect $ 870.00 minus any commissions

First, you need to know that the futures options go off the board in the second week of the month preceding the expiry; so the expiration date for the July options for coffee is on June 9. Assume that coffee opens the Monday after expiration at 130. Here is what would happen: The July 100 call would be worth 30 points or $11,250. The two 110 long calls would be worth 20 points each, or $15,000. The 120 call would be worth 10 points or $3,750. The worst-case scenario is that the entire butterfly would zero out, just costing commission plus the $870 per butterfly we originally took in.

Let's go the other way: Say July coffee opens the Monday after expiration at 90. The most we can make on that trade is $870, minus commissions. What if the Monday after expiration, coffee opens at 105? Ah! We are short the 100, so it would be a cost of $1,875, plus commissions. Why? Because our original long position would be worthless and, although we took in $870, we would have a charge against that of $1,875, which is a loss of $1,005, plus commissions. Wherever the market settles between about 102.5 and 116, we will have a loss. Think of the butterfly in this way: Your 100 call is covered by the 110 call and your 120 call is covered by your other 110 call. Thus, you are short the 100/110 call spread and long the 110/120 call spread. The short call spread in which you sold the 100 call but bought the 110 has a maximum loss of $3,750 per call spread at expiration. The long call spread in which you sold 120 calls but bought the

110 has a maximum gain of $3,750 per spread at expiration. It is your hope that this trade closes above the 116 area; actually, you really would like to see a close at 120.

Short Butterfly

The preceding trade is a long butterfly; but you can also trade a short butterfly. How would that work? You would now be long the 105 call and the 115 call and short the 110 calls. In this instance, you would like the market to close at 110 or 109. Why? Because you are long the 105 call at a cost of 198.75 and it will be worth $1,875. This is your best-case scenario.

Buy 105 call at 8.93	$3,348.75
Sell 110 call at 6.57	$4,927.50
Buy 115 call at 4.74	$1,777.50
Cost	$4,927.50
Proceeds	$5,126.25
Net	$ 198.75
Maximum loss: $1,875 − $198.75	$1,676.25
Maximum gain: $1,875 + $198.75	$2,073.75

Would I do this spread? In a word: *no!* Here it is simply used as an example of a butterfly in a market, chosen purely at random. Frankly, in a trading range market, I use different sorts of strategies. In that same market (i.e., July coffee), I do not believe the market to be easily capable of going to the 130 level. Also, I don't believe that this market is going to self-implode. My first task is to look for juicy options. A juicy option is one with meat or premium in it. In commodities, the options with the most meat are coincident to the expiry of the futures. What that means is that the options in the months without futures contracts may be good for purchases but not really great for sales. Coffee has an expiry in the May, July, September, December, and March months. If I were to sell an option, it would be in those months. However, were I to buy an option, it would be in the odd months without an expiry.

So, how did I decide that the market was range-bound? I looked at the chart. In Chapter 4, we discussed trending markets and various tools that you can use to find markets and to analyze the direction, or probable direction, of the markets. Most important, you must look at the trend. You also should review the weekly and perhaps monthly charts. This is important information for you to obtain, if you are going to put your money at risk.

When I looked at the daily chart of July coffee (Figure 9.1), I noticed that the market seems to be going sideways after suffering a downtrend.

FIGURE 9.1   Daily chart of July coffee. (Copyright © 2006 eSignal. Published by eSignal, www.esignal.com.)

This means that, although there has not been a vigorous rally in the product, by going sideways coffee has broken the downtrend line. Now that is interesting. However, coffee has not started a move to the upside and appears to be building a base. The weekly chart does not agree with that finding, but it illustrates to me that the lows are higher, even though the highs are not higher. In other words, we seem to be coiling, or getting ready for a move. If you draw a downtrend line from the top of the rally in that market and then draw an uptrend line under the lows of that market, you can project out into the future as to when these two lines will likely meet. Should the market stay confined between those lines, we know from past behavior that a violent collision will occur. (See Figure 9.2.) Even were we to calculate out into the future and solve for the collision of these lines, it won't matter. Why? Because by the time these lines collide, the contract will have expired. Now we can feel confident in finding options that will work best in this scenario, one of a trading range-bound market.

Although there is a frost warning about the blooming coffee trees, it is the same warning every year and still no frost. Eventually there will be frost and the market will go crazy on the upside, so you should keep that possibility in mind when tooling an option strategy for that market.

FIGURE 9.2 Weekly chart of July coffee. (Copyright © 2006 eSignal. Published by eSignal, www.esignal.com.)

BACK TO BASICS (MAKING MONEY)

The goal of any trading strategy is, naturally, to make money. The amount of money to be made is directly correlated to the risk you are willing to take. I am not a great risk taker and rather prefer happily plodding along, rather more like the turtle than the hare. Once you have learned how to do this, you can choose to also plod along or to take the riskier, faster road.

There are several ways you can trade this market. One is delta neutral trading (covered in Chapter 8). As you recall, a delta neutral trade keeps the position flat. When the position is looked at it is neither long nor short; it is simply flat. Remember, with options, you must babysit the position to keep it neutral daily. The market may push you to the long or short side and this has to be removed if you want to be delta neutral. Delta neutral trades are the preferred method for most professional options traders. Some of us who have options will tilt that option trade in favor of the direction we believe that market will go. This sort of behavior flies in the face of the professional options trader who essentially doesn't care where the market is going. Having come from the equity side of the market, I continue to have an opinion.

Here is what I did in July coffee. I sold three times as many calls as I bought futures. Actually, the trade started out as twice as many, but I had to adjust it so that my position would not be overly long. I sold the 130 calls and bought the July futures contract. As an equity trader, you probably are saying that you have sold a covered call. In futures, when you sell a covered call, you are thought to be long the put.

That is not a typo. Let me explain to you that when you own the future and sell the call, you have a position that would be the same as if you were to sell the put. Still lost? If you were to sell the put, you would collect money for that obligation and you would be long should the market decline. Isn't that the same as a covered call? Welcome to option-trader-speak!

Back to July coffee. I bought the future and sold three calls, which at the time was a somewhat neutral trade. When I entered this trade, I paid 115 and change for the futures and sold the calls for 4.10. At that time, I thought it was possible for coffee to go to the 124 level, but felt that it was so overbought that it would take a while to muster enough strength to move to that level. While waiting, the options I sold would enjoy the erosion of time. Remember, should coffee start to rally, I will have to buy more futures contracts. As coffee sells off, I will become longer and thus be able to sell more calls. An alternate trade is to calculate how low this market will go before a bounce will appear. On that side of the trade, I chose to sell the 97.50 puts and buy the 92.50 puts, for a credit of 1.00 per put spread. I am risking 5 points, but feel that this trade is worth the risk. Add that to the 4.10 per call option and you have a nice return on limited risk. Notice I was not afraid of the upside, but rather of the downside.

Debit spread versus credit spread: A debit spread costs you money and a credit spread pays you money; that is the difference between them.

CONDORS

A condor is a variation of a butterfly. The difference is found in the long/short calls. The strikes of all four calls are serial and differ. This is the way it would look for IBM:

July Condor Long

Sell IBM 75 call	9.20
Buy IBM 80 call	(5.42)
Buy IBM 85 call	(2.30)
Sell IBM 90 call	0.75
Cost	($772)
Proceeds	$995
Net	$223

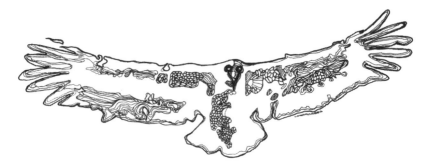

Condor.

or:

July Condor Short

Buy IBM 75 call	(9.20)
Sell IBM 80 call	5.42
Sell IBM 85 call	2.30
Buy IBM 90 call	(0.75)
Cost	($995)
Proceeds	($772)
Net	($223)

This trade would cost you $223. Remember that these trades are without the cost of commissions, which can eat into your profits. Inasmuch as you are doing a four-footed trade, you must use a deep-discount broker to get these executions. All of the numbers are real, not made up.

Both of these are condors: one is a long condor, and the other is a short condor. Let's do the math. Remember, this strategy is for trading range markets and works best in that environment.

What happens if the market closes at 83, which is where it is today?

The 75 call would be a debit of $800.

The long 80 call would have a value of $300.

The other two calls would be worthless.

You would have lost $500 on that trade. No, you collected $223 so your loss plus commissions would be only $277 per condor.

What happens if the market closes at 85?

The 75 call would be a debit of $1,000.

The 80 call would have a value of $500.

The 85 and 90 calls would again be worth zero.

Loss on the trade would again be $500 minus $223 or $277 per condor.

What happens if the market closes at 87?

The 75 call would be a debit of $1,200.

The 80 call would be a credit of $700.

The 85 call would be a credit of $200.

The 90 call would be zero.

Credit is $900 and debit is $1,200; thus you have a loss of $300. But remember, you earned $223 with this condor; so your cost is $77 minus commissions.

What happens if the market closes at 90?

The 75 call would be a debit of $1,500.

The 80 call would be a credit of $1,000.

The 85 call would be a credit of $500.

The 90 call would be zero.

That trade is worth zero.

What happens if the market closes at 95?

The 75 call would be a debit of $2,000.

The 80 call a credit of $1,500.

The 85 call a credit of $1,000.

The 90 call a debit of $500.

You are again at zero.

What happens if the market closes at 75?

The 75 call is worth zero.

The 80 call is worth zero.

The 85 call is worth zero.

The 90 call is worth zero.

You made $223 on that trade.

Now let's reverse the trade, and sell the middle and buy the wings. At 75 we already know that the proceeds will be zero. At 80 we will have a profit of $500, but we have to remove the cost of buying the condor, which is $223; profit is $277. At 85, we have a gain of $1,000 from the 75 call and a loss of $500 from the cost of the short 80 call, and the 85 and 90 calls are both worthless; thus, we have $500 minus $223, which was our cost, for a $277 profit. At 90, we have a little different picture. We have a profit of $1,500 on the 75 call, a loss of $1,000 on the 80 call, and a further loss of $500 on the 85 call; again, the 90 call is worthless. That whole trade is worth zero.

The best way to trade a condor in a trading range market is to sell the middle and buy the wings. It costs you money, but your total risk is worth that reward. Buying the spread isn't really a good trade.

WINGS

Wings are the options found at the end of most chains. They continue to have a value of pennies and deltas approaching zero. Many people like to sell these options because they have only a remote chance of having any value. I believe that it isn't worth the event risk to sell these cheap options. You would be better off buying these options.

TREES

Yes, they do grow in Brooklyn. In this strategy you buy one call option and sell two or more against that long call position. In reverse, you can sell one option and buy several options above or below that short option. Let us look at the trade. Say I am long the Russell 1000 700 call; to complete my tree, I sell the Russell 710 call and the Russell 720 call. What do I want? I want the market to basically stay in a range so that I can collect on the short calls and make money on the long call. The Russell September futures contract is trading at 697.

Buy Russell August 700 call at 12.65.

Sell Russell August 710 call at 7.30.

Sell Russell August 720 call at 3.70.

This trade will cost me 1.65 to put on.

I am hoping that the Russell 1000 will stay in a range and actually close near 710. Why? It's simple: I am long the 700 call for 1.65, not bad unless the market moves out of its recent range. With this position, I do have almost 10 points of protection. Remember I am long the 700 call and short the 710, so if the Russell rallies to 712, I am still making money. At that point, I would have to go long a futures contract because of the upside liability. If I sold the 700 call and bought the other two calls, I would collect 1.65 but I would have to be long some mini contracts to cover my risk on the upside. The Russell 1000 has mini contracts that trade at the New York Board of Trade. A mini contract is one-tenth of a regular contract. These minis help the options trader to control risk without overhedging.

PACKAGES

Packages are combinations of put spreads or call spreads, one of which will be a ratio spread. The easiest way to show you a package is to give you an example of one. Again we will use the Russell 1000 contract for this example. The Russell still is at 697.

Buy one August 690 put at 7.80.

Sell one August 680 put at 5.55.

Buy one August 670 put at 4.05.

Sell two August 660 puts at 2.95.

The trade will cost me 0.40, but if I increase my ratio on the 660 puts I will collect money. Many times we move the ratios around a bit so that they work better. Much of the time the package needs to have two months to be priced to more of your advantage.

Here is an example of the same trade just going one month further into the future. I would opt for this rather than paying for the trade.

Buy one September 690 put at 9.60.

Sell one September 680 put at 7.40.

Buy one September 670 put at 5.70.

Sell two September 660 puts at 4.40.

This is a credit package that would give me 0.70 in my account. What is my risk? Should the market crash, I will be in a bit of pain.

CONCLUSION

Butterflies are beautiful and so are condors. These are two strategies, along with the tree and the package, that you can use in a trading range market. We will be looking at further complications to these very simplistic options in the next chapter.

What I have illustrated is that in the creation of different kinds of combinations of options, as the writer, or seller, you can calculate with certainty how much you can make and how much you can lose. The illustrations show you that you can make money and do so without exaggerating your possibility of a huge loss. This is a good risk management technique with a twist. Remember for every position you can think of there is somebody out there with the opposite goal. It is not as though you are being different but you each are satisfying your objectives. When I sell an option, I don't know who is buying it or why they are buying that option. I can only imagine that they have an agenda of their own in which my option plays a role.

CHAPTER 10

Using Options in Reversing Markets

This chapter outlines methods for offsetting negative movements in your position. Note: I said negative movement positions. The implication is that you might be either short or long, but in either case the market movement is giving you grief. Yes, options can be utilized in this situation as a modality for working yourself out of a problem. Often it might be easier to just close out the position and take the loss, but there are times when—with patience and a little creativity—you can work yourself out of a bad situation and neutralize the loss probability.

In my years as a trader/hedger/analyst I have often been called upon to get people out of a mess. Usually, it is some sort of crisis that caused the mess but many times it can be as simple as a loss of judgment for a second or two. There was one instance in which I thought I was short and bought to cover that short only to find that I was flat. Once having made the error, I fixed it by using options to exit the trade. In this chapter we will look at a long in a declining market and general blowups that happen, even to smart people. In this chapter you will learn about packages, backspreads, and synthetics, all of which can be used to correct for a problem or as behavior in a reversing market.

I can cite a personal exposure: Immediately after the 9/11 terrorist attack, my portfolio suffered its own attack—initially because the markets were closed, and again upon the implosion seen in the market prices. I could have taken an additional hit, but because I was already damaged by the market, I chose instead to save some positions from total loss and was actually able to neutralize those losses. While it wasn't possible to save the entire portfolio, a substantial portion was recovered by rolling and moving options around. No one of us is so informed as to anticipate the unforeseen dangers lurking in the the vast prospects of the future. Many of the lessons I have learned were costly, but valuable to the learning curve. It is my objective to offer the experience gained at such a cost so as to spare you some of the anguish I endured in suffering the expensive losses I have sustained.

REVERSING MARKET EARMARKERS

A market that is about to reverse and go down is not one bit disposed to sending up flares saying, "Sell me!" But these markets do sometimes give you little clues that all is not well, although, more usually, the clues are hidden inside a raging bull market, destined to become the Great Bull Trap. In Chapter 4 you have learned how to identify a trend. This very elementary technique can help you save thousands of dollars.

COMMONSENSE RULES

Here are some rules that I use in trading. These rules did not come cheap; most of them cost me real dollars to learn. Some of the rules have been passed to me by others, but as usual, I had to see if they were true, and they are. Many say rules are made to be broken. Believe me, these have been expensive ones to learn.

Rule 1: Don't Tell the Market Where You Want It to Go; It Will Tell You

As simple as that sounds, it is difficult to persuade some that the market is the leader; we are the followers. As the market marches on, say to the upside, you are getting some clues that the rally might be in trouble. What are these clues? Well, one clue is that the volume on the up days is not as good as it should be. The volume should be robust and constant. In a failing market, the volume increases; it lightens up on the advance. Thus, you have lower volume on the way up and greater volume downward into the troughs. This may be the precursor to the eventual lower lows that you will be anticipating.

Rule 2: Look for Lower Lows and Lower Highs

Don't try to trade in a contra-direction. Most of us who are traders seeking to enter the market look for a contra-trend entrance. In a reversing market, this can be a painful experience. If you do want to trade in that manner, then watch your stops so that you don't lose too much on the trade. If you are at the point where you are praying for a reversal, you are in trouble.

Rule 3: Wait Until You See the Whites of Their Eyes Before You Put Out Your Options

Many times, traders fold under the weight of their options positions and simply buy them back at the market price. We, in the ring, have a crude descriptor for this behavior: puking. When traders are puking, sell them back their options. How will you know when that occurs? In the ring, you will see it off the floor. You will notice that the prices being posted are higher than they should be and that the volume increases. This is a good time to accommodate the trade. In the ring we often hear a broker ask, "Where can I buy these back best?" or "Where can I buy these best?" The broker in this case is trying to get the best price for his client's order rather than asking where the market is and just saying "Buy them." The specialists in the ring will make a two-sided market that is a buy and a sell price, like "50 bid at 90." What that means is that they will pay 50 or sell at 90; it's your choice. Fair value is somewhere in between those numbers. It is the specialist's goal to make money on the trade—to buy below fair value and sell above fair value. That is a market order, which in the Russell ring is not common.

Rule 4: Reversing Markets Don't Send Out Messages

When a rally reverses, you will see multiple attempts at renewed rallies, all of which fall short of the mark. This leaves something on the chart that looks like a rounded mound. This is that point where you must pay close attention, because unless a rally can take out the recent highs, the market will likely go down. Look for rounded mounds in topping markets.

Reversing markets from a sell-off are generally of several types; for example, you can have the V bottom or a protracted period of time in which the market seems to be going sideways, albeit with microscopic rallies. The latter chart looks rather like a saucer, or a rounding bottom. (See Figure 10.1.)

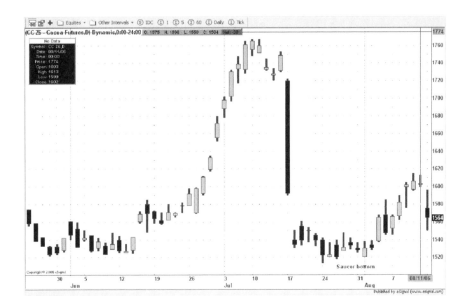

FIGURE 10.1 Saucer Bottoms. (Copyright © 2006 eSignal. Published by eSignal, www.esignal.com.)

PRICING MULTIPLIERS

Equity options have a multiplier of 100; if I quote an option at a price of $2, I really mean to say $200 ($2 × 100 = $200). OEX options on the S&P 100 index have a multiplier of 100; if an option is priced at $2, it is $200. Russell 1000 and 2000 options have a different multiplier, which is 500, so if I quote you a cost of $2 on the Russell, I really mean $1,000 and not $2 ($2 × 500 = $1,000). The S&P 500 has a 250 multiplier, which means that the option priced at $2 is really $500 ($2 × 250 = $500). Or take coffee options, where the multiplier is 375. That option, if quoted as $2, is really worth $750 ($2 × 375 = $750). Each market has its own multiplier, which can be found on the exchange web page. The New York Board of Trade (NYBOT) lists these as well as the margin on each contract. The New York Mercantile Exchange (NYMEX), Chicago Board of Trade (CBOT), and Chicago Merchantile Exchange (CME) all list the multipliers as well as the margin requirements as set by the exchange. Margin is set by your brokerage house, but can never be lower than the exchange's minimum; it may be—and it usually is—higher.

EUROPEAN VERSUS AMERICAN STYLE OPTIONS

U.S. stock options, or American style options, can be exercised or assigned at any time, up to and including the expiration date of the option. This may create difficulty for the option investor, should part of the package be removed. Package in this case refers to a combination of several options together in one trade that was put in place. I showed an example of this in Chapter 9. For example, if you have a call spread that you are short and the long calls are exercised, you can suffer a greater loss that you might comfortably tolerate. Such an experience is not unusual in an overnight exposure. When you are told of such an exercise, it may be too late in the day for you to close out the other half of the spread, leaving you exposed overnight. Should the stock be the subject of a hostile takeover, you might have reason to worry. When that activity occurs, I usually suggest that the position should be flattened or that some other adjustment should be made to remove the risk.

Futures contracts are usually settled in the American style, but there are some traded here in the United States that are European style so in those instances you do not have to worry about an early assignment or an exercise. However, with futures, you do have the basis for a worry over a weekend following the expiration of those options. For example, say you were short the 110 May coffee calls and the Friday session closed at 109.90; you could arrive on Monday morning to find your account to be short the May contract and to have the exposure on the upside. Of course, you can easily remove that risk. There might be another instance where, if the market closed at 109.80, you were short the 110 put and expected assignment, but the holder abandoned the option, leaving you waiting for the futures contract.

Assignment and exercise are random. With stocks, if you have in-the-money options, you must instruct your clearinghouse or brokerage house of your intention to call away or sell. With futures, you must instruct your clearinghouse to abandon your options, or it will automatically exercise or assign the futures. The equity assignment is randomly done by the Options Clearing Corporation (www.optionsclearing.com), which notifies the brokerage house of the number of options that have been exercised or assigned. Then, the brokerage house will assign the securities to your account. Sometimes this is done in a first in, first out (FIFO) manner and other times it is just done randomly.

Sometimes futures options, such as the S&P 500 and the Russell indexes, have morning settlements. These options are settled only after every stock in the index is opened on the third Friday of the quarter: March, June, September, and December. You may have to wait until mid-morning to learn if your option is viable.

Stock options that expire on Friday settle by noon on Saturday. The brokerage house will have the stock in your account by the Monday following the expiration.

OPTION STRATEGIES FOR REVERSING MARKETS

I have been very successful in making money in reversing markets by using a combination of options that actually create a credit. For the down market, a put package that is crafted from the starting point of buying the higher-strike put is used. This is a valuable lesson that I learned from 9/11. In the past, it had been my custom to sell out-of-the-money puts and perhaps buy the puts below those options for some safety. During 9/11, these unlikely puts became the albatross around my account, causing a huge loss. To be clear, it was my fault. However, I did learn an important lesson: Now I always buy the higher-strike put and sell the lower-strike put.

Put packages can be crafted easily, especially when the volatility increases, but they work in low-volatility markets as well. The first task is to find the value of the beginning put that you want to purchase.

Let us say that you want to put a Russell 1000 package on. The Russell 1000 is trading at 711 today.

The 680 put for May is trading at $2.00.

The 670 put for May is trading at $1.10.

The 660 put for May is trading at $0.60.

The 650 put for May is trading at $0.30.

The plan is to buy the 680, sell the 670, buy the 660, and sell the 650 puts and collect a credit, or do it for zero. If you put on a ratio spread, you could collect some money, but let us see how it works out.

The spread should be a $1 \times 2 \times 3 \times 6$.

Cost for one 680 put	$2.00
Payment for two 670 puts	$2.10
Cost for three 660 puts	$1.80
Payment for the six 650 puts	$1.80

You can do the spread for a credit of a dime.

Here is what expiration could look like:

- Should the market close anywhere above 680, the package is worthless and your dime is safe in your hands.
- Should the market retreat to the 680 level, you are a happy camper because you are on the money with your put; although it is not worth anything at this juncture, you have collected a dime.
- Should the market retreat to the 678 level, your happiness is increasing by the day. You own an option that is $2.00 in-the-money and the rest of the package is worthless. Your proceeds from the trade will be the original dime plus $2.00.
- Should the market retreat to the 674 level, elation is beginning to set in. The rest of the package that you have crafted is worthless. But your 680 put? Well, it is worth $6.00. Your proceeds are $6.10.
- Should the market close at 670, your joy is almost impossible to contain; you have made 10 points on the credit spreads. Additionally, the 670 put is worthless.
- Should the market close at 666, you are beginning to fade and are getting worried. Your long put is worth $14, but your short puts are $4 in-the-money, and you have sold two of them. Don't worry, because 14 minus 8 plus your original dime still gives you a profit of $6.10.
- Should the market close at 660, you are certain that you are in deep trouble, but luckily you are not. Your 680 put is worth 20 bucks and

your short 670 puts are now a minus 20 (so the trade is worth zero), and you still have the original dime.

- Should the market close at 656, things are getting a bit clouded. Now the 680 put is worth 24, but the 670 put is worth 28; you are losing $4 on the trade. Relax, remember you bought the 660 puts; they are now worth $4 each and you have three of them, so they are worth 12 bucks for a profit of $8.10.

   The 680 is worth 24 (1 times 24).

   The 670 is worth 28 (2 times 14).

   The 660 is worth 12 (3 times 4).

   The 650 is worth zero.

- Should the market close at 644, here is what will happen:

   The 680 is worth 36 (1 times 36).

   The 670 is worth 52 (2 times 26).

   The 660 is worth 48 (3 times 16).

   The 650 is worth 36 (6 times 6).

You have a loss of $4.00 (minus your original dime, for an actual loss of $3.90).

Of course, as the markets drop your loss escalates, but you have a lot of time in which to make adjustments to that trade. The market needs to sell off 71 points for you to begin to feel the heat on this trade.

This trade can be adjusted in many ways by changing the ratios. Further, there is nothing stopping you from removing the legs of the trade, should you feel so inclined. I have enjoyed putting these trades together. Standing in the pit with really smart people helps educate one in some of the methods employed by the better traders. This is an example of a trade originally done by a friend called Perma-Bear. I tweaked it a bit, but it was he who introduced me to the art of the package.

BACKSPREADS CAN BE FUN

Backspreads are your basic ratio spreads. In equities, an example of a backspread would be to purchase four IBM July 75 calls and sell one IBM July 70 call. These trades are difficult to find because your goal is to put on a trade that will not cost you money. Basically, you are looking for the in-the-money call (or put) to pay for a multiple of the out-of-the-money call (or put). The example just given is of a call backspread. For a put backspread, you would sell the 85 put and buy four of the 80 puts.

It is important to note that I am using the 85–80 put ratio spread only as an example—it doesn't work in today's market in that issue. It takes a great deal of effort to find backspreads that work. Ideally, you would like to have a 1 by 4, but in many cases, you simply can't find them and would have to settle on the less profitable 1 by 3.

Why are backspreads so much fun? Simply because they limit your risk to $500 per spread and the upside on the calls is unlimited. Of course, the upside on the put is limited to the value of the security in question. You can only go to zero, remember, so if a stock is selling for 65 and it goes to zero, your profit, although huge, is limited by the distance the stock will travel to zero. In contrast, if this is a call spread your upside is not capped by anything except the value of the security. Just imagine if you had done a backspread on Google at 100.

Veeco Instruments is trading at $23 per share. If we sell the July 20 call, we will get $4.50. If we buy the 25 call for July, it will cost us $1.10. By selling one in-the-money call, we can pay for four July 25 calls and actually collect a dime.

Sell one July 20 call and receive $4.50.

Buy four July 25 calls and pay $1.10 each or $4.40.

What happens if Veeco closes at 23 in July? We will lose $3.00 on the trade. If Veeco closes at 25, we will lose $5.00 on the trade. Remember to multiply that number by 100 to obtain the value of the trade. Should Veeco close at 15 in July, we have lost nothing and have collected a dime. Should Veeco close at 30 in July, the party is about to begin. Actually, the party starts when Veeco closes above 27 and it gets better as the prices rise.

At 30, we are about to have a ball. While we are short the 20 call and it is worth $10, we are also long the 25 calls, which are now worth $5.00, and we own four of them, so although the short call is going up in value, our long call position is more than offsetting that debit. As a matter of fact, if you look at the position, you are short a call spread and long calls. At 30 we have four calls that are worth $5.00 each, so it looks like 4 times 5, which is 20. The original short call is worth $10, but we have calls worth $20 so we have made $10 without spending any of our own money. We have a limited downside risk and an unlimited upside potential.

On the put side of Veeco, we sell the 25 put, collect $2.50, and buy the 20 put for 45 cents. We can do this one five times: sell one 25 put and buy five puts with the money we collected. Our risk is $500 per ratio spread. Say Veeco had a bad earnings report and the stock, at expiration, is trading at 15. We have a liability of 10 from having sold the 25 put, but we have a credit of 5 times 5, or 25, from the puts we are long.

This is an example of a put backspread.

There is nothing stopping you from putting these trades together in many different combinations. As a matter of fact, I frequently buy one option when I perceive it to be cheap, and layer other options on top of the original. Then there are times when I just put the spreads on as a package and execute them as a package. Obviously, you cannot do this as an online trader because you frequently need the prices to reflect the credit for the spread or the debit for the spread you are considering. Professional traders place orders in that fashion. In other words, they calculate the cost of one leg minus the credit of the other leg and because there are two options rather than just one, they look for a slight discount for executing both sides at the same time. They leg them only when they have to—it is cheaper to do it as a package. Often I include the equity in the package as well. This is especially true when trading the Russell 1000, Russell 2000, or S&P 500 options and futures. At the New York Board of Trade, we are able to price many legged strategies in this manner.

SYNTHETICS

In a reversing market, you might want to have a position that would benefit from the change of mood in the market. You can create a position that is a synthetic long, or a synthetic short, without ever buying or selling a stock.

Synthetic Long

To create a synthetic long position, you simply sell a put (that makes you long) and also buy a call (that makes you long as well). You have synthetically created a position that will benefit you in a rising, reversing market. You have also reduced the cost of this trade by selling the put to finance the cost of the call. The maximum downside can be measure by the strike price of the put you sold. Say you sold an 80 put on XYZ for July, and XYZ goes bankrupt. What is the maximum you can lose? Eighty dollars per share. Since one option is worth 100 shares, your maximum loss is a possible $8,000. Suppose now the stock is the subject of a takeover and it runs to $300 per share. You bought the 85 calls, so what is your investment worth now? Three hundred dollars times 100 is $30,000! There is no upside limit to that trade.

Synthetic Short

You might want to participate in a droopy market by creating a synthetic short. This is done by selling the call naked and buying the put. Your loss is unlimited in this trade because you are short a call. Should the market on that stock go up, as XYZ did in the previous example, you will have a huge loss. On the positive side, should XYZ go to zero you will have made 80 times 100, or $8,000 on that trade.

CONCLUSION

When a market is reversing, it is difficult for many traders to abandon the previous trend of the market and many live in hope for the return of the old trend. Markets don't care that you are losing money. The best advice is not to fight the market. Instead, identify the new direction and then craft an options strategy to help you benefit from this reversal of tides. Backspreads, synthetic long/shorts, and packages help you take advantage of a reversal of the mood of the market. As with all options trading, it is critical that you quantify the risk and take measures to insulate your trades against adversity.

PART III

Managing a Position

S o here we are with tons of knowledge at our fingertips. Now what do we do? First, we need to learn how to use these strategies to our own advantage. This begins with explaining what a hedge is and how to use them; you will find that information in Chapter 11. These hedges are very basic and they will begin to open your imagination to the what-ifs of options trading. Chapter 12 will help you understand how you can use this new skill in managing a truly awful trade. Here you learn a few tricks. Remember, these tricks are limited only by your own imagination, so have fun with this chapter. Managing a winning position in Chapter 13 helps you get the most out of a winning trade. Chapter 14 pulls the whole book together, showing you how you can use these new and imaginative skills.

CHAPTER 11

Fundamental Hedging Strategies

Now that you know what options are, it is time for you to learn how to use these tools in managing positions. Options offer you flexibility not seen in other instruments. Hedging and managing a position encompass skills associated with risk management and risk removal. Hedging is risk removal. For example, you could buy stock in Home Depot and sell stock in Lowe's, and that would be a sort of hedge. This hedge is called pairs trading, or selling the weaker and buying the stronger but staying in the same industry. When using options you are able to deflect problems, speculate, and invest with some degree of certainty as to the risk of the position and the reward. This method is far superior to pairs trading in that you are using the derivative of the instrument that you want to trade.

Hedging is meant to remove or reduce the risks associated with trading strategies. Assuming that this describes an arbitrageur would be a grave error. An arbitrageur trades on price inefficiencies, whereas a hedger, in hedging a trade, seeks to deflect a perceived risk from that trade—all the while making money. No one willfully hedges away his profits. That would be a hedge that doesn't work. But a genuine hedger is interested in keeping his position neutral and otherwise really doesn't have a market opinion. This is a hard concept for some to accept, but it is true. When you ask a true hedger what he thinks about a stock, a future, or a bond, he will tell you that he has no idea and, further, that he doesn't really care.

In this chapter we are going to explore some of the easy hedges, which will help you to learn the hows and the whens you will need to remove the risk from the trade. These are simple easy ways to deflect some of the risk associated with trading. There are many fancy names for what they are, but it is more important to learn how to use them rather than what to call them. I can tell you that you will learn about fences, and trees.. The good news is that we will describe the hedge and not bother you with the exact name of what it might be. The names aren't going to make you money; the trade will. So that is exactly what we are going to concentrate on.

To repeat, hedging is meant to remove or reduce the risks associated with trading strategies. Note the drawing of someone bending over the market to illustrate the flexibility that options provide the trader.

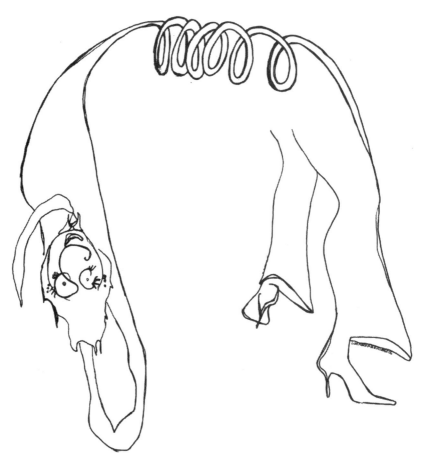

The picture is of me having to stretch my imagination in an effort to create a position that will be both profitable and have limited risk. Thus, you see I need a spring to move and flexibility to get there. Oh, the high heels? They are just for show! Who could wear heels while trading, anyway?

THE SIMPLE TRADE

Simply speaking, the easiest hedged trade is to buy a stock and to buy a put. Such a position has unlimited gain possibilities without loss risk up to the expiration of the put option. How does one come to that conclusion? Very simply; you buy a stock primarily because you believe that you will make money on the trade. Then you buy a put. Now, remember, a put is like an insurance policy for a specified period of time. Thus, you have removed the downside risk of the trade. All you then have is the possible upside. If the stock goes nowhere by expiration you haven't lost much (just the cost of the put option), and you should sell the stock or purchase another put to continue your protection. Alternatively, you can short a stock and buy a call; this will protect your upside exposure. When you short a stock or other security, you are hoping for a retreat in the security; by purchasing a call, you are protecting yourself against an upside surprise. This protection will last only to the option's expiration date. After that date, it will be necessary to redo the option or to flatten out the position. Of course, it is understood that both the put and call options would be close to the price of the long or short. This is a very simple yet useful hedge for a position.

Here's a demonstration of how this hedge works. You buy 1,000 shares of Home Depot. You pay 41.25 for the stock, which has a volatility of 32.90. Next, you buy an August 40 put at the cost of 1.25; thus, your cost of the trade is really 41.25 plus the 1.25 you paid for the put, or 42.50 per share. Now your trade, which cost you $41,250 for the stock and $2,500 for the option, is an almost totally hedged position, with a loss possibility of 2.50 (42.50 cost minus 40 strike price), which is 2.50 times 100 or $250 per option; further, remember that you bought 10 options to cover your 1,000-share trade, so your cost outlay is $2,500; that is your total risk on a trade, worth $42,500. Remember, each option is worth 100 shares and you need to protect your purchase of 1,000 shares; thus, you have to buy 10 put options.

What happens if the stock rallies to $50 per share? Your stock is now worth $50,000 and you will have a very lovely profit of $50,000 minus $42,500, which is $7,500 for the trade. Okay, say the stock closes at 40. Well, the put will be worthless and you will lose $42,500 minus $40,000, which is a loss of $2,500.

Now say the stock goes to 30 per share. What is your loss? Again, the loss is $2,500 because you own the 40 put and will put your shares to the holder of the put.

Now let us look at the call side of the equation: You short the stock at 41.25 and buy the 40 call for August at 3.20. The call is a bit more expensive because it is an in-the-money call. The short gives you a credit of $41,250.

The cost of the call is $3,200; therefore, you will have a profit of $41,250 minus $3,200 (cost of the call), or $38,050. Say the stock goes to $50 a share; okay, here is what will happen: You will sustain a loss of $1,950 on the trade. How did I do that? Well, you bought the 40 call, so anything over 40, up to the expiration of that option, doesn't matter to you because you are protected. Now imagine that the stock drops to $30 a share; your profit will be $8,050 on the trade.

All of these numbers are valid until the expiration of the option, at which time the hedge will be gone. You need to either redo the options or flatten the position and move forward. Another cautionary note is that no commissions have been included in these calculations and, although these prices are real at the time of writing this book, they may be different in the future. These are randomly chosen stocks for demonstration purposes only.

THE HEDGED TRADE

Anyone familiar with covered calls will tell you that the trade is hedged. Frankly, I will tell you that the upside is spoken for; however, the downside risk remains a liability. Think about IBM again. (I don't mean to single it adversely, but it is easy to talk about.) Say you sold an in-the-money (ITM) call and now you are sure that you are safe. But you are not safe if the stock retreats below that call.

Let's get more aggressive and sell a deep in-the-money call at 40 when the stock is selling at 41. That trade is not hedged. It is a remote liability, but a liability nonetheless. Say you wanted to sell the 40 calls for July that expire this week. You would receive 42.10 for your efforts. That is 1.10 over where the stock is today; after commissions, you would be in a losing position. Going further out on the curve, what happens when we go to the July expiration? The first thing we notice is that there are no 40 calls; rather, they are 45, so back we go to April to solve for that. The July 45 calls are selling for 37.50. The 37.50 proceeds from selling the 45 calls plus 45 (the proceeds received when the stock is called away from you) equals 82.50, not a lot of money for holding that position until July. By holding the position until July, you will capture a dividend. The April 45 calls are selling for 35.90, so 37.50 minus 35.90 is the time value of that option, or 1.60 for two months of risk. It is not likely that IBM will lose half of its value in the next two months, but the risk does exist, so just to be safe we could buy the 45 put for a nickel and remove the risk from the trade. Do we care where IBM is going to be in July? No. If you want to be cute, you could buy the IBM 45 call for 35.90 and buy the stock at a discount to today's value of the stock. So, here it is: buy the April 45 call for 35.90 and sell the July call for 37.50 and buy the July 45 put for a nickel. You will be buying the stock at a discount, selling the calls at a premium, and buying the protective put for almost nothing. That is a hedged trade.

STRADDLES

A long straddle is a purchase or sale of both a put and a call with the same strike price and the same expiration. An example would be buying or selling an IBM 80 call and an 80 put, expiring at the same time. Why would you want to do this? Well, assuming that you don't know where the market is going to head, but are fairly well convinced that it *will* move, you might want to purchase this call and put on IBM. The gamble here is that the stock won't move from its current price of 81. In this trade, you are positive gamma and positive theta; the theta part is your enemy because that is a measurement of time erosion. Inasmuch as you are long or betting that the market will move and you have purchased options, your position erodes with time; thus, time is your enemy. Theta, a measure of decay of the option, is the enemy of a trade that is long options. What you are betting on is an increase in the volatility of this stock. Should the stock remain stuck in the mud at 81, you will lose money on the put and lose money on the call. Because you are long the call option, you are long gamma. Gamma is the rate of change of the thus delta; it is a second-order derivative.

If you are long the straddle, you want the market to move in either direction and you want that move to affect the prices of the options. A trader might buy a straddle on a stock that is due to announce earnings. She would expect the stock to react to the earnings announcement with a big move, up or down. She doesn't care which side it is, just so that it moves. One side of the straddle will be trashed and the other side will make money, enough to pay for both put and call and put some money in your pocket.

The other side of that trade would be to sell the straddle. Many option traders like to sell the straddle when the volatility blows to the upside. They do this in an effort to cash in on fear. As a straddle seller, or a short straddle, you are short gamma and short theta. One side of that equation will work for you, so long as the volatility doesn't blow out to the upside. When you are short theta, you are watching your short options erode, day by day. You can actually calculate how much money the position is making you on a daily basis. In the case of IBM selling at 81, you will be short the puts and short the calls, both at 80 for the same expiration. The money you collect for taking this risk is yours; however, this is not a hedged position and it will protect you only to a point. Let us solve for how much you will be protected.

Start with the volatility of the underlying asset, IBM, which is 37.90. We are going to sell the 80 calls and sell the 80 puts for April (you don't like to do straddles too far out; keep your expiration month close at hand). You get 2.45 for the call and 0.65 for the put. That is a total of 3.10. That is exactly how much protection you have on the upside and on the downside of the trade. Should IBM trade at 83 by expiration, you will have made a dime on the trade. Should IBM go much higher, you will lose money on the trade. As to the put side, so long as IBM is above 80, you will make money on the put side. Your points of protection are limited to 3.10 points; thus, you are protected to 83.10 and 76.90. Anything in between these numbers and you will make money. So, how do you hedge it? By buying the stock as the market rises or selling the stock as the market drops; this means you must pay constant attention to that trade. If you use the next option cycle as the target of your straddle sale, yes, you will be paid more money, but you are agreeing to more time for the stock to rally or to retreat and increasing your risk. Why? Because the less time to expiration, the less likely the stock will move that far. There is another way to look at this and that is to say: The less time until expiration, the less time the stock has to make a move and thus your risk increases. Many futures traders get annoyed when the risk managers at the clearing firms blow up the margin as expiration approaches. Simply, that is because there is less time left for wiggle room and thus your risk is greater.

STRANGLES

Perhaps you would like to strangle *me* at this point with these crazy options, but hang in there! Strangles are selling or buying both puts and calls for the same expiration, but not at the same strike price. (It doesn't have to be an equal number of puts and calls, but it usually is.) If you are long the strangle, you will be buying a call and buying a put, both expiring on the same date, but with different strikes. Generally, strangles are comprised of out-of-the-money (OTM) calls and OTM puts. Visualize a rope around the position and you can see a strangle. That is a long strangle. A short strangle is selling OTM calls and OTM puts with the same expiration date but with different strikes. The goal of selling the strangle is to collect the premiums of both the calls and the puts. You do have risk on this trade, but the risk is far less than that of a straddle. At the same time, you are being paid less money for the risk you are about to take. An example of an IBM strangle would be a purchase of the 90 call and a sale of the 70 put. The call will get you a dime and the put will give you a nickel. You are not being paid much, because you aren't taking much of a risk. Remember, the higher the risk, the more you will be paid.

THE BOX

Simply put, a box is a combination of a synthetic long and a synthetic short position. What is a synthetic long? It is owning a long call and selling a short put. The call is your right to own the stock and the put is the buyer's right to sell you the put. Both options have the same expiration. A synthetic short is a position where you have sold a call and bought a put; thus, you are short via a naked call and you are short having purchased the put. Both of these positions have the same expiration. The combination is called a box.

If we bought the Home Depot August 40 call for 3.20 and sold the August 40 put for 1.25, we would have a synthetic long position. Should the market rally, we have the privilege of buying the stock. Should the market retreat, we will be put the stock, both sides, resulting in ownership of the security. If we sold the August 40 call for 3.20 and bought the 40 put for 1.25, we would be short. Because we are naked the call, we have to deliver the stock if it is in-the-money at expiration and we have to sell it at $40 a share. We bought the put, which would give us a right to sell the stock, again making us short. Generally, this sort of box is not at the same price, but the expiration is always at the same time.

IRON BUTTERFLY

This is a truly hedged position. You are long/short the strangle and long/short the straddle. Say you are long the Home Depot 40 call and long the 40 put; you are long the straddle. Then you would sell the strangle, say the Home Depot 30 put and the 50 call. What you now have is a call spread and a put spread, which is called an iron butterfly.

It is a lot easier to look at it as a call spread and a put spread. You can reverse the position and sell the straddle and buy the strangle.

THE WINGS

Many times you will hear professional options traders speak about either buy or selling the wings. The wings are far out-of-the-money (OTM) options with almost no (and in many cases, no) delta. A wing can be a put or a call; it doesn't matter. These options have little probability of risk, and therefore you are not paid much for them. Most professional options traders therefore will not *sell* wings because, even though the probability is slim of these options having value, there is far too little reward in the trade and the margin that would be tied up is certainly not worth it. Rather, options pros buy these cheap insurance policies. We on the floor call them atomic bomb options. As an aside, just one threat of an incident and whoosh, these options become valuable. I have seen this happen on several occasions in the past. There is a prominent local on the floor who has a special program called the PPP trade. What is that? you ask. The perpetual put program.

VERTICAL SPREAD

This is simply a call spread or a put spread, either long or short. Vertical spreads are in the same month but at different strikes. For example, if you are long the IBM July 80 call and are short the IBM July 85 call you are long a vertical spread. If you were short the July 80 call and long the July 85 call you would be short the vertical spread. If you bought the July 80 call and sold the July 85 call you have a debit vertical spread. Why debit? Because you had to pay for the spread, simply because the lower-strike call costs more than the higher-strike call. A credit spread would be selling the lower-strike call and buying the higher-strike call.

CALENDAR SPREADS

Since we are talking about spreads, let's also look at calendar spreads. Say you are short a call with a strike price of 85 and expiration of July and also say that the stock or future is trading near that strike and you are approaching the expiry month. What many do is to deflect some of the pain from the trade by purchasing the current short call and paying for it with a call in a month that is further out, say August, along with a higher strike. You stall the trade another month and you buy some more room on the upside. Many traders try to do this for a credit, which means you would get paid to do the trade. That is a calendar spread.

It works the same with puts and calls. Many combinations are put on to fund a purchase of a sold option gone bad. In other words, the option you sold is beginning to blow up in your face and you are looking at the barrel of a rifle. Well, maybe that is a bit of an exaggeration, but that is how it feels. You can put off the pain into the future by buying back that option and selling an option with a more favorable strike price further out in the future.

Sometimes you might have to sell another option to create the position. Here is an example: Say you are short the Russell 2000 July 730 calls and the index is now at 724; obviously you are not a happy camper because this option is about to blow up in your face. You have several choices in this matter. You can buy back the option and move on to the next trade, you can start to buy futures to cover your short options position, or you can buy back the option and pay for the trade by selling a combination of options or a single option. The trade in which you would buy back the call and sell a put to pay for it is called a risk reversal. The call is viewed as a risk, and selling the put, for some unknown reason, is viewed as less risky. (As an aside, that isn't really why they call it that.) So, you buy the July 730 call and sell the July 690 put to pay for it. I just made up the strikes as an example. It may be that the option will need more than a naked put to pay for it and that is when we get combinations to pay for things.

Similarly, you can buy the July 730 call and sell the July 690 put and August 620 put for a credit. Getting the idea?

CONCLUSION

Options offer you lots of ways to neutralize your position, not as a defensive move but rather as an initial position. Hedges are easy to establish, especially if you want to do them at a specific price. Many times, it is possible to get a quote on an entire package, say buy the call spread, sell the put spread, and sell the stock short. Market makers will price the entire transaction for you. One word to the wise: Get quotes on all the pieces so that you are aware of what the price should be if you did the whole thing separately. Then, expect to have a better price for all the pieces in a package.

CHAPTER 12

Managing a Losing Position

It's remarkable how creatively a trader can adjust a position to minimize the effects of finding himself on the wrong side of the trade. No trader ever wants to lose, and many doggedly hang onto a losing position in the forlorn hope that the market will vindicate them. Some traders believe in cannonballing, which is the act of adding to a losing position in an effort to average down one's original mistake. Cannonballing is not a preferred trading method; rather, it is the antitrading method! Why, then, would a trader cannonball? Because the market needs to move a smaller amount to get the trader out even. This may seem reasonable, but if the trade idea didn't work initially, why add to futility?

This chapter explores ways to work your way out of a bad position. While the smartest trade is probably to take the loss and to move on, many cannot do this. We will, therefore, explore some of the ways to make the bad trade better—perhaps not great, but maybe good enough to get yourself out of a mess without having to take the loss. Most of these creative option methods are on-the-spot creations intended to fit a specific condition, but the same type of thinking applies to most of such problems' solutions. The short gone bad was taken from a single day's trade just as an example. I simply looked at the most advanced price list and took the highest price percentage gainer for that day and there it was, my short gone bad example. True, it wasn't the best cover but it was a good reduction of loss by the use of options. Look at the drawing on the next page and notice the sweat on the trader's brow.

Flexibility and stress are the earmarks of a trade gone bad. Absolute imagination and creativity are needed to remove problems as they crop up so that the dollars don't disappear. And yet with all this advice and knowledge there is a degree of stress. Notice the trader is drenched in perspiration, fearing the loss of his money with this trade gone bad!

ANATOMY OF THE BOO-BOO

You are a portfolio manager and you're falling behind your peers in the gains on your assets. You take a calculated risk and are suddenly faced with a three-point loss in a day. Clearly, if your boss sees this mess, he will destroy you. What do you do—confess to your boss and beg for forgiveness, or get clever? Many go with the get-clever trade and try to pretend that the error was a planned trade. Not to suggest that you deceive anyone, but your objective is to get out of a mess without taking the loss. This scenario was brought to my attention about a year ago by a manager who had just traded the Russell 1000 and was three points on the wrong side of the trade. It didn't take terribly long for that position to blow up, just a couple of hours. And that error worked out to be a $1,500 error per contract. So you can appreciate that, when talking about 10 or 20 contracts, we are clearly *not* talking about chump change. When I got the "Help!" phone call, it was late in the day and the plea for help out of this mess was frantic.

Sadly, all too many traders panic when a trade goes against them and they become immobile, unable to think; they just sit, frozenly staring at the quote screen rather than perhaps just taking the loss philosophically and moving on to concentrate constructively on the next trade. Then there are those who, once having made the error, try to compensate for it by overtrading and by taking unnecessary risks. This usually compounds into a bigger mess. I believe that once the error has been made, it is a timely and wiser idea to analyze the reason that initially prompted the basis for the trade. One would hope that you bought the object because you believed that the market was heading in some specific direction. Or were you just shooting craps and had no prior reason for either buying or selling? If that is the case, shame on you!

This is real life we're talking about, with real possible losses. Always have a real reason for doing whatever it is that you are going to do. This book began by painstakingly showing ways of finding the direction of the market and for studying that direction—all of which should be done before the trade is made.

So, back to our friend with the three-point loss on the Russell 1000. He pleaded with me to give him some idea of how to fix his mess without taking a loss on the trade. Actually, I came up with several ideas; however, I suggested only the best one. When viewing an error or a bad trade, looking at all the options is always a good idea. This particular trade was a painfully long position. It could well have been a painfully short position, but this time it was a long. The very first thing I consider is how to solve the problem of getting out of the trade, should it go further against me. Obviously, in this case of a long position, I started the problem's solution by looking at a possible put purchase.

In Part Two, I said that buying a put is rather like buying short-term insurance. Unfortunately, this is going to cost money. The reason I started with the put in this situation is that the put purchase would stop the bleeding on the loss side of the equation. One can come up with several puts worth looking at. Once that is done, you have to look into paying for that purchase. Many times, I choose to pair the orders so that the entire package is done at one time. Why would I do that? Simply because I don't want to take any further risk on that position; I want both sides done at the same time. In that way, I am locking in both the cost and the funding of that cost simultaneously, removing further market risk.

In this case, a put was purchased for downside protection, but because the market was falling I had to find a put that was away from the purchase price of the future. The put purchased was four points below the long entrance and thus, assured the investor of an additional four-point loss on the position. What I did next was to solve for the calls. I had to make up the four-point put cost and the three-point error loss. I looked at the calls and found that if I were to sell a call, not too far away from the original purchase price, I could take in a substantial amount of money, although not enough to make up for the booked loss. What I did next was a little creative. I discovered that if I sold two calls for each long, I could take in enough money to pay for the put and to make up for the loss on the futures contract. Thus, the trade became a sort of ratio trade. I further had to place a good till canceled (GTC) order to purchase additional futures should the market rally beyond the call strike price. That order was to be canceled upon the expiration of the options sold.

THE TRADE

The basic idea of our example shows what happens when you believe that the market will rally and, just to spite you, the dumb thing falls! (Of course I must admit that the market really doesn't care what I think or you think; it does it own thing.) So you bought a futures contract with the belief that you would make money on that trade. (Why else would you buy an index?) The object of your purchase was the Russell 1000, which you purchased at 641. Let us further say that you traded the Russell 1000 and went long a contract at 641. The market immediately fell apart and dropped three points (or handles, as they are called, 1 being the handle). Now you are long a futures contract at 638 and have a paper loss of $1,500. Immediately, you can sell a call against this poor purchase. You would look at the May call and collect a premium of 8.35 (in dollars, this is $4,175). Now you seem to have a covered call on this bad position.

What you have done is reduced your cost of the futures contract by 8.35. A pit trader would tell you that you were "short the put" (long a futures contract and short a call). So, what you want to do is to purchase a put to limit your downside risk, or just sell the futures contract and buy as many mini futures contracts as is dictated by your delta, which, I would guess, is about 0.44. There are several ways to hedge this position. One is to sell a multiple of calls, equivalent to hedging your position completely. Thus, if the delta is 0.44 on the option and you are long a contract, you need to sell two calls to neutralize that position. Delta can be defined as the risk or the probability of the trade going to that specific price; obviously, the chances are pretty good for that strike price. Going further, say you don't want to sell your futures contract. Okay, then buy a put in addition to selling the calls. This will limit your drawdown on the trade. I suggest that in this instance, you might purchase the 634 put, using up some of your premium received for the calls. The delta on the put is –0.4241. So let us do the math: Add 0.44 and –0.4241; the answer is 0.0159, which means that you are short a fraction of a mini contract. You have removed the risk of the trade. You cannot make more than one point on the upside and you cannot lose more than four points from the close or the time at which the hedge was employed.

Here is what happens if the futures go to 644: You make one point on the futures. Say the futures go to 630; you bought the right to sell the futures at 634, ensuring a 7-point loss on the trade. There is yet another way to hedge this position, and that would be to sell the futures contract and buy five minis instead of selling the additional call.

Here is another example. Say you bought the Russell 1000 futures contract at 717.25 and it is Tuesday, April 25, 2006. Let us agree that the futures contract closed the session after Ben Bernanke's speech at 714.25. Based on that close, you would have a three-point or $1500 loss on the futures contract. Okay, here is the repair: First buy the put you will need to stop the bleeding of cash on the downside. (At this point we don't care if the market goes up or down—we simply need to stop the loss.) We can purchase a 714 put that will expire in May, at 7.70. If we want, we could purchase the June 714 put for 11.35. Next we look at the calls. We can sell a May 718 call for 5.90, or sell a June 718 call for 9.40. In either case, we will have to sell twice as many calls as we own futures. Let us use one contract just to make life easier. Here is the trade. Compare both months to decide which will be the better trade:

May Trade

Buy one May 714 put at a cost of 7.70
Sell two May 718 calls; receive 5.90 × 2
Cost of put $3,850
Payment $5,900
Net $2,050
Three-plus weeks to expiration
GTC buy one future at 718

Buy one June 714 put at a cost of 11.35
Sell two June 718 calls; receive 9.40 × 2
Cost of put $5,675
Payment $9,400
Net $3,725
One month plus three weeks to expiration
GTC buy one future at 718

With the May expiry we have only three weeks left to worry about the position. We have removed our downside risk, but we have an upside risk. June expiry will expand that risk to the futures contract expiration month. At the end of that expiry, we will have no position, because the futures will settle for cash. With the May expiry, we will have to deal with the futures contract to flatten the position. Further, with the June contract we will make more money along with taking on the greater risk.

Here is our worst-case scenario:

Should the futures contract go to zero we will make $550 on the May option cycle and we will make $2,225 on the June expiry. On the upside, should the market go to 800 for the May expiry we will make $2,050 plus 75 cents on the futures contract (.75 times 500 or $375) or $2,425. For June the numbers are $3,725 + $375 = $4,100. If the contract closes anywhere below 718 we will have to sell the futures contract for the May expiry or just let it settle for cash in the June expiry. In either case, we will be ahead of the game. The danger in this game plan is that it is possible that the market would gap open higher on a day, electing the GTC order, and we might get a fill at a higher level. That would remove some of our profits.

The other huge difference in the softs is that you can offset your position right there in the pit. You actually can, in the case of the Russell 1000, 2000, currencies, and commodity indexes do it in the same ring as the futures trade in. Thus, you can get the whole job done in one place. This is not to say that you can't do something like that in equities, but when you put in a net trade in equities, you have to use a trading desk to get the deed done for you. On the floor, you are able to negotiate the entire package. If you made an error and the market didn't go up as expected, you can sell/buy the next expiration, reducing your risk and your margin. Then, if things go your way, you can either sell or buy the spread as a single transaction, or can just lift a leg of that spread. A spread is said to have two legs: March could be one; May could be the other, or any combination of months you might choose. You will be long one and short the other. Why? Say you believe that the market in coffee is going to go down. Usually, the front month has more violent swings and higher open interest than do the other months, so it is not unreasonable to believe that May won't drop as quickly. Thus, if you are short March and long May, you are taking advantage of the decline, or hoped-for decline, in March with relatively little movement in May. When you cover, if you do one side without the other you are said to be lifting a leg of the spread.

Here's another example. You are short March, long May, did the spread for a differential of a positive 2.80 points. (The difference in the price of the two contracts traded: March is 117.00 and May is 119.80, so the spread will be 2.80 bid at 2.70.) The reason for the strange-looking bid and ask is this: If you want to buy the spread, you will be buying March and selling May, so you will have to pay the offering price for the March contract and sell the May contract to the bidder. Effectively, you are paying more to buy the spread than you would to sell the spread. Now, you are short March. You can further repair that position either by selling March puts or by buying March calls. Let us assume that the price of March coffee is 117 and that you sold the 115 put for March. Selling that put gives the buyer of that put the right to sell March coffee to you at the expiration of that put. You don't care—you are already short March coffee, so that would flatten your position. Traders usually like to take in premium rather than to pay it out. So, let us continue. Say, instead, you bought a 115 call for March. This also flattens that side of the spread. Recall that you are short March and long May; well, now you would be simply long May. Why? Because buying a March call removes the upside risk of the trade while keeping the downside profit potential open. To solve that, you could sell May calls or buy a May put. The other obvious solution is to simply close out your May position. Here, we can play with numbers so that we can take losses and repair them. I would suggest that futures might offer a bit more flexibility in the trade.

OPTION REPAIR SOLUTION

Over a year ago, I was dragged into a repair of an Elan trade gone sour. Elan is a pharmaceutical company whose stock plummeted when its multiple sclerosis drug was pulled from the market. That news event caused the stock to crater, sending the shareholders scrambling for cover.

While many of our brethren would have you buy the dip by way of stock or options on these fallen angels, we do not believe that stock slammed by bad news is wisely repaired by such strategies. Perhaps a wiser course might be to continually sell calls on issues, applying some of that premium to buy protective puts. It is analogous to buying short-term insurance against loss. Once a stock has been hit with an affecting news item, it can usually be purchased for a turnaround bounce the next day, but then get out! In Elan's case, this stock opened at 26.76 and closed at 8.00 on Monday, February 28, 2005. The most you could have realized from that dead-cat-bounce trade, would have been 50 cents—not worth the trade. About a week after the plunge, you could have bought that issue for 5.71. The low print for the move was 5.53.

Let's look at the options: Say that you bought the stock here at 5.71; you could sell the July 7.50 calls, receiving a premium of 1.00, and buy the July 5 puts at a cost of 1.05; thus, if the stock is called away from you at 7.50, you have made two bucks on the trade; on the downside, you can sell the stock for five bucks in July. You risked 76 cents on the trade; not a bad risk/reward. Actually, the stock would have been called away from you in July.

Now let's look at this another way: Say you bought the April 5 calls at a cost of 1.35 and that you bought just as many calls as you had shares in the company. Then, you sold the April 7.50 calls, but twice as many as shares you were long (you have a core position and just doubled it synthetically with options). You are totally covered; what would happen here? Cost is $1.35; that is out-of-pocket; sale is 45 per option, but you sold twice as many, so you are collecting 90 cents and you have no downside protection. That won't work. While you'd make a possible $2.50 per option, plus the 90 cents (a total of $3.40), removing your cost of $1.35 leaves you with $2.05 ($2.50 profit on the appreciation of the stock, minus $1.35 cost of the call option, plus 90 cents premium received for selling the call). Buying downside protection will cost you 60 cents, to buy the April 5 puts. Remember, you have to buy double to be totally protected; that's at a cost of $1.20. This strategy will give you $2.05, minus $1.20, or 85 cents in your pocket, if the stock is called away. If the stock closes below $5.00 on the third Friday of April, you will have lost 15 cents, plus you are out of your original position. While your risk is that the stock will go to zero without the protection, you are already mortally injured by the drop in that stock, and remember you are agreeing to sell it at 7.50 in both scenarios. Why look for more trouble? We don't care what kind of premium you took in during your investment in that security; that plunge was a killer. On the dead-cat-bounce theory; don't stay there and don't wait for the comeback.

We are, of course, speaking of Elan. At these levels, don't bother buying calls; if you want to gamble, and we mean gamble, buy the stock at these depressed levels, sell the calls, and buy the puts for insurance. Options are very flexible in their ability to help manage positions, but sometimes the cost of all this maneuvering is too high. The preceding scenario will work and is based on real closing numbers, but the question is: Was it worth it? We did not include commissions in this example; once they are added, your costs escalate.

A SHORT GONE WRONG

The previous example was for a long position gone bad. Now let's look at an example of a short position gone bad. For this example I chose Office Max, which was up 12.56 percent or 4.25 in a recent trading session. This issue was picked from the most advanced price list without any prior

> **Note**
>
> A good till canceled (GTC) order is an order that remains on the books un-
> til you cancel. There is another type of order that I use regarding stocks: a
> GTC, DNR, which in English means good till canceled, do not reduce. Why
> do I do that? Because with stocks that pay dividends, that order will be re-
> duced by the dividend payment. Because these orders are price specific, I
> don't want that order reduced; therefore it is placed as a GTC, DNR.

knowledge of this company. If you shorted the issue yesterday and now
find yourself 4.27 in the hole, what can you do? Obviously we shorted the
issue at 33.32 and now it is at 37.59. The first thing we need to do is to
look at the June 37.50 calls, which are selling at 1.90. Our primary concern is to stop the hemorrhaging on this stock by buying enough of these
calls to cover the short position. If we shorted 100 shares we would need
to buy 1 call; if we were short 1,000 shares, we would need to buy 10
calls. Next we have to find a way to pay for this, so let's look into the 40
calls and the 32.50 puts. We can get 1.45 for the 32.50 puts. By selling
these puts, we are going long the stock at 32.50. We are also being paid
1.45 for taking on that obligation, which reduces our costs for the calls
from 1.90 to 0.45.

We have now locked in the maximum loss on the trade and also have
locked in the maximum gain on that trade. Right now, that would be a loss
of 4.27 plus 0.45. That does not make us happy, so let's move further. The
40 calls for June are selling for 65 cents. We can sell those calls and take in
the 65 cents to defray the cost of the 37.50 calls. We are risking another
2.50 points, but we are willing to take that risk. We will automatically put
in a GTC order to buy the stock at 37.50 plus 0.65 or 38.15 until that June
option expires. We would also consider selling more puts with an additional GTC order to sell the stock should the market drop to 32.50. This is
a repair that almost works.

What happens if the stock closes at 39? We lose the original 4.25, but
we make an additional 65 from the 40 calls, plus we sold twice as many
puts, creating another 1.45 per contract. Say we sold 100 shares short originally. Now we have to adjust the position to reflect one call spread and
two put spreads:

Long calls: 37.50, at a cost of 1.90.

Short calls: 40.00, paid 0.65.

Short puts: 32.50, paid 1.45 twice.

Long puts: $30.00, paid 0.05.

GTC order: buy stock at 38.15.

GTC order: sell stock at 32.40.

1.90 minus 0.65 = 1.25 = call spread.

1.45 minus 0.05 = 1.40 = put spread.

1.25 times 1 = 1.25.

1.40 times 2 = 2.80.

We paid 1.25 for one call spread.

We were paid 2.80 for two put spreads.

Net: 155.00.

At 39 we lose on our 40 calls, but we have locked in the maximum loss on the short sale of the stock at 37.50; thus, we will be stopped out at 37.50. The puts we sold are worthless and we collected $280. Thus we lost on the short but reduced that loss to 3.37 from the original 4.27.

Even if the stock goes to 45, we don't care. We are long the stock, and the most we could lose on the options is an additional 0.65 per share.

Let's say that we just bought the calls and didn't sell the higher strike. We would have ended that trade with a loss of 3.37 instead of the 4.27 originally seen. We were able to reduce the loss by 25 percent with that trade and we did not increase our exposure.

Now, let's say that the stock drops to 25. Do we care? Not if we had a GTC order in to sell 100 shares of the stock at 32.50. Why not 200 shares? Well, because we were already short 100 shares from the original trade and we only have to cover for the additional put to keep the position flat (that made us long; remember, we are now long 200 shares). We would have made money on the short from the 33 level to the 32.50 level.

This isn't a good example, but it was chosen from the most advanced list so we could illustrate how this could work. True, we didn't remove the entire problem, but we reduced the loss by 25 percent at the worst and could even have made money in the best-case scenario.

What we did here was to cap the possible loss, restrict the possible gain, and remove some of the shortfall. Now, if the stock closed at 35, we would be free to place this trade again in another expiry, further reducing the loss.

Let's look at another stock: Home Depot. Say we shorted Home Depot at 40. What can we do to protect ourselves on that short? Keep in mind that when you short a stock that pays a dividend, you will be charged for that dividend should you be short on the ex-dividend date.

The 40 call for June is 1.70. The 40 put for June is 1.10. We are short at 40 and could actually cap the possible loss at 1.70 by buying the 40 call. We would like to make money on the trade and would feel good about covering the stock at 37.50; thus, if we sold the 37.50 put for June, we could get 30 cents. That would reduce our possible loss from unlimited to 1.40 per 100 shares. Now, if we are right and the stock drops, we will make 2.50 per share, so we are risking a loss of 1.40 to make 2.50. I'll take that risk if I feel that the stock will drop.

CONCLUSION

Options open the door to creative thinking in which you can measure your liabilities and possibly fix your errors. Although it appears that the futures arena is friendlier to this sort of bobbing and weaving, it is possible to construct a decent hedge in the equity arena. It seems that there is more flexibility in futures, but when you are in need of an options fix, you can find them lurking about in the equity markets also. If you make an error, consider correcting that error quickly by just simply taking the loss and starting all over again. There is something to be said for a clean slate; however, if that is not possible, look to the options to help you fix your errors. Some of the most creative projects have been accomplished because of an original error.

CHAPTER 13

Managing a Winning Position

Until now, we've been concentrating on learning how not to lose in our market decisions. Is having a winning position a matter for concern? Actually, it is. There's no question about the desirability to make correct choices, but more important is the objective served: to keep the money that your hard work has earned for you. There are several ways by which to accomplish this. Most investors feel a compulsion to eke the last cent out of the investment and would hold on until their winner becomes a loser.

The goal of this chapter is to help you overcome the "could-have" and "would-have" segment of the trade and show you how your trade profits can be kept for at least a while.

THE WINNER

Everyone would have loved to be long Google at the initial public offering (IPO) price of $85. Now that the stock is trading well above $400 per share (it has traded well below that level also), those nervous investors who sold the stock at $200 might harbor some regrets that they took their profits early rather than let them ride. If truth be told, their choice was probably correct. It is easy to say that, and there are other things that could have been done to allow a greater appreciation in that security. There is, of course, more than one way to solve this problem. One way is to take half of the investment off the table—just sell half of your shares. In the case of Google, you would have your entire investment returned to you while continuing to own the stock. Another simple alternative would have been to place a floating stop. The stop is noted as floating because you'd have had to adjust it at every 10 to 20 points of advance on the stock, keeping that stop wide enough to avoid getting stopped out of the long. A good rule is to put a 10 percent stop-loss limit order in on a stock. If you lose more than 10 percent, you want out of the stock. There are other ways to accomplish the same objective, alternatively, using options.

THE COVERED CALL

Selling a covered call means you are long the stock and are selling someone the right to buy that stock from you in the future at a specific time and price, capping your possible gains. Now, if you are unwilling to give up on the upside, there are ways of adjusting this position to have it work for you. Yes, you can sell a covered write, but you can employ the use of a backspread, just in case the stock runs further to the upside. Remember the backspread. We sell the lower-strike call and take the money and use it to buy a multiple of the higher-strike calls.

Let's consider an example: Airgas, a company that is up about 65 percent through the middle of 2006. This company will do well in an economy that is expanding, as it produces industrial gases, acetylene for welding tanks, and the like. We look at the options and discover that we could sell the July 40 call and collect $2.70 per option ($270). At the same time, we could purchase the 45 calls for a cost of 70 cents ($70). That is an almost 1 to 4 backspread, but we would use the 1 by 3, take the change, and buy a put. I would consider selling the straddle, or both the call and the put. The call would be a covered call and the put would make us long. I would consider doing this in the October expiry. Why? Because we can collect $5.10 for the obligation and then buy the October 35 puts for a cost of $1.05 ($105), which would cap our possible loss. If the stock rises, who cares? We sold the stock we were long. If the stock falls, who cares? We are long the puts, under the naked strike, which put $4.05 ($405) in our pocket. Loss is a possible 95 cents ($95); gain is at least $4.05 ($405); not too bad. If you continue to be bullish on the stock, you could buy some calls above the sold call: say, sell the 40s and buy the 45s, just not to lose the upside.

EMC is a company that has been stuck in the mud for about a year. This stock has an option strike at every point, so you can sell the options where you want to. Unfortunately, with a stock like EMC, you won't get much in the way of premium for the options. The low for EMC has been at the 13 level, the high at 14.75—not too exciting. No wonder the options are so flat. In this instance, you could sell the 13 put and sell the 14 call and collect the premium of 75 cents ($75) for the exercise. Is it worth it? Probably not, but it is feasible.

One of my favorite stocks remains Trinity Industries. This issue has rallied from the 40 area in December 2005 to 64.15 just five months later. Because this security has enjoyed a robust rally, its options will reflect a little more volatility than options of less volatile issues. With the stock at 64 and change, we could sell the 70 calls for July for 1.65 ($165) and also sell the 55 puts. By selling the calls, we are capping our upside, but we are being paid for that privilege, today. By selling the 55 puts, we are going long the stock at 55. I would love to buy this stock at 55. We are managing the upside position by preselling the stock. We should buy the puts rather than sell the puts to wrap up the trade, but because I like the stock I would like to add to the position. This is an easy way to do that.

Another stock I like is Tractor Supply Company. This stock has also enjoyed a robust rally and is at the upper edge of its trading range. Rather than worrying about the rally's continuance, I'd prefer to sell some options on this stock. I could sell the July 70 call for 1.45 ($145) or sell the July 65 call for 2.95 ($295). With the money, I could buy a put for 1.80 ($180) and rest easy, knowing that I am safe until July. If the stock goes higher, great, but should the stock fail to continue its rally, I won't care.

Here is another stock that I have liked for a while: Eastman Chemical, which traded to the 56 level. The stock shows that there is more upside to this rally. What to do? If I sold the September 55 calls, I could collect 3.30 ($330) and then, if I sold the September 55 puts, I would get paid another 2.65 ($265), collecting a total of 5.95 ($595). I could then purchase the September 50 puts for a dollar ($100). In a worst-case scenario, I would lose a nickel ($5). But I have to hold the stock until September. Best case? I make 4.95 ($495) and still own the stock and can do this exercise again. Risk a nickel, profit 4.95; an okay risk/reward trade. Oh, by the way, I also get the dividend on a stock with a price-earnings (P/E) ratio of 8.04 and actual earnings with growth.

Joy Global is another of my favorite stocks. This one has a major volatility issue and it pays you well for trading the options. The stock is at 65.55 today. The volatility is 48.36; therefore, the options have nice returns imbedded in them. Say, we were to sell the July 75 calls; we could get 3.00 per option ($300) for selling that call. If we were to sell the 70 call for July, we could get 4.90 per option ($490). But remember that I like this stock, so I might consider selling a put on this issue. Let us again look at the possibilities. I sell the 70 call and take in 4.90 per option ($490); then I sell the July 65 put and take in an additional 4.40 ($440), but just in case it doesn't work, I buy a July 60 put at a cost of 2.55 ($255). I have taken in 9.30 ($930) in premiums and paid out 2.55 ($255), giving me 6.75 ($675) in my pocket today; of course I get the dividend as well. I am protected below 60 and have a risk of five points between the two puts; but remember, I have taken in 6.75; therefore, even if the stock declines to 60, I make money. What happens on the upside: I lose the stock at 70 dollars per share in July. The premiums are mine to keep; so my actual profit is 70, plus the 6.75 I earned from the premiums, plus the dividend. Not a bad return on my money.

WHAT DO ALL THESE WINNERS HAVE IN COMMON?

In a word: volatility! As the volatility increases, the premiums in the options increase, reflecting the increased rate of change in the prices of the underlying, thus giving us the opportunity to take advantage of this condition. As volatility increases, we become option sellers, rather than option buyers. Professional option traders really don't have an opinion on the market; rather, they have an opinion on the volatility of the market. Thus, when the market attains extremes in volatility, a condition that has been absent in the market for a while, we become natural sellers of options. As the volatility collapses, we become buyers of options. That is just how it works.

MANAGING A WINNING SHORT SALE

Yes, shorts can be wonderful moneymakers, especially given the velocity of retreats when compared with the velocity of advances. Why do you suppose the futures pits in the financials are usually short? The answer to this one is a two-parter. First, retreats are generally faster and more violent than are the advances, so you can make more money on a good short than can be made on an equivalent long. Second, futures traders like to sell the front expiry in the futures contract and to roll them each quarter. Why? Because they want to earn the premium between the cash and the futures price. They are making money as the futures price approaches the cash price. The futures price is calculated using dividends received and interest rates earned in the calculation of fair value. Thus, if the futures contract for June are selling at a five-point premium to cash, the futures trader will want to capture that money with the full knowledge that, by expiration, the futures will equal the cash value. The risk of an upside explosion or a downside retreat can be offset with options, as you have already learned.

A short position can be managed by a purchase of calls because it caps the possibility of a loss by giving the purchaser a right to buy the issue at a given price. Since the short needs to buy an issue to close out a position, a purchase of the calls will do that. In addition, the short can also sell the puts on the issue; this is another way of getting long or stopping out the position. By selling the puts, you put more premium into your account, but that action does not remove the upside risk of the position. Only a purchase of the issue, or a purchase of calls, will do that. Remember, however, that if you purchase calls they too will expire, leaving you open to an unlimited loss. It would be a good idea to close out the position when the options expire.

Say you were short Bausch & Lomb Inc at 62.01, just before the news of its ReNu contact lens product problems hit the market. It is now trading at 43.97. Besides patting yourself on the back for having been a genius, you need to consider closing out that position in a way that lets you keep the lion's share of the gains you made on the loss in the stock. If you bought the May 45 calls, they would cost you 1.55 per share—not an awful price to ensure the financial gains you have already made. Further, consider selling the 40 puts for 65 cents, so as to partially pay for the calls you need to buy. This exercise will cost you 90 cents ($90). Should the stock drop further, you will be out of your short position at 40; remember, selling the put makes you long. At that point, you can either sell the calls you are long or hope for a rally so that you would make money on the upside. Frankly, I would close out the position if the stock drops further, using the short 40 put to exercise the cover.

It is important to know that the put you sold can be exercised at any time until expiration. Unfortunately you have to wait for the holder of the option to put the stock to you. Be sure that as the stock drops the put owner will look to unload his position in the underlying stock, freeing up cash and possibly reducing margin in that account. These are American style options; that allows the holder to exercise at any time, up to and including the expiration date. (European options can be exercised only at the expiration date.) We have capped the amount of money that we can earn on the continued decline of the issue, but there is a saying on Wall Street: "Bulls make money, bears make money, and pigs get slaughtered."

Try to remember that one.

CONCLUSION

While it seems to be a no-brainer to manage a winning position, options play an important role in enhancing your ability to keep your gains. I have shown you how to manage a winning long position, as well as a winning short position. These techniques are not terribly creative, but they are very useful methods of keeping the money you earned in your pocket, ready for the next trade.

CHAPTER 14

Pulling It All Together

Very early in my career on Wall Street, I learned that hard work would be necessary to distinguish me from the masses of others in this industry. I entered the board room to discover that I was one of two females employed as brokers. True, there were plenty of females in the support staff, but there were only two gal brokers. That never bothered me, especially after my interview for employment wherein the interviewer told me to go home and have children. Basically, I told him that I had already done that and that I was now faced with supporting my three offspring. He just kind of shook his head and glared at me and asked about my husband's support for the children. I explained that he was a bankruptcy lawyer and he looked bankrupt, so the burden of the lion's share of support fell on me. I was hired.

When I started in the business professionally in 1981, the market had double-digit inflation, double-digit money market yields, and very little reason for anyone to invest. Further, we in the investment field were still fighting the bad feelings left by the 1970s and the gun slinger mutual fund era. So, I became a pro at finding good stocks with great upside potential. How I did that was really not that hard, but at that time, before the Internet, it took a lot of research and reading. I became a subscriber to Value Line publications and scoured their ratings and reports on companies. I continue to be a subscriber to those valuable publications. This is where my research began. I set upon finding fundamentally sound companies, then looked at their charts, and voilà, a stock pick was born. I must also add that in that era we used blue and green chart books because there were no laptops and Internet charts.

We had to use publications that were published weekly and overnighted to the office. Of course commodity charts were updated daily and sent to the office daily.

I started this book with the objective of showing the technical basis for successful markets trading. This chapter brings together all of those different aspects of trading we have discussed into a final, cogent form. In truth, we all know that we do not live in a bubble, that even a true die-hard technical analyst, myself included, will necessarily admit that in every investment there needs to be a happy marriage of both fundamentals and technicals. The balance sheet does count, earnings are important, and growth is also an important factor. There are far too many stocks to look at without the use of filters; therefore, use them to sift out the junk and to allow you to focus on the ones that remain.

USING FUNDAMENTAL ANALYSIS

You have to start someplace in wading through the thousands of issues available to purchase or sell in the market. The fundamental information you obtain has been supplied by the company in the case of a bond or a stock that is being studied. All of this information, like balance sheets, cash flow statements, and debt, is important, but remember the source of that information; it is the company that is supplying it to you. In futures, it could be supply/demand, warehouse stocks, weather, and the economy that will influence the fundamentals to be studied.

I use fundamental analysis to help me find candidates that meet certain criteria that I have set. I insist on earnings; no wish and a promise for me. I want growth in a company. I would like to see a dividend as well as insider ownership in the company. The book value, price-earnings (P/E) ratio, pension liabilities, preferreds, debt, and so forth should all be on the lean side. In other words, I don't want to see heavy pension liabilities sitting on the balance sheet. These are obligations that will have to be paid and that will impact earnings. I like to see good coverage on the company's debt and intelligent use of debt.

Going Long

I can sense that you want to cringe right now, but I require myself to look at what a company is all about before I consider investing in it, even if the chart is outrageous. There are certain factors I examine that help me filter out the junk while retaining the good stocks. Here's a rundown of these factors.

Earnings   Earnings do count. It is nice to have a business in which people invest that makes no money, but to me and the IRS, after five years such an exercise is a hobby, not a good investment. This is one of the filters I use: The company has to earn money in its ongoing business. That means it needs to make money from its ongoing operations. The reason I emphasize limiting this to cash flow from operations is that it is possible to make money from investing and other operations that are unrelated to your business unless, like Berkshire Hathaway, that is your business model. Further, when I limit this to the cash flow from operations, appreciated assets, which can inflate the balance sheet, are removed.

Price-Earnings Ratios   There must be a reasonable valuation for the stock. Again, it sounds elementary, but P/Es do count. To solve for them, one simply takes the current price of the stock and divides it by the current earnings. I like to see these numbers within some reasonable level. If the company produces so much cash that it has free flow from cash, great. Free flow from cash is the excess in cash produced by the business after all bills and obligations have been met; this includes dividends! It also makes me happy to see a company that pays a dividend.

Insider Ownership   If the insiders don't own their own shares, why should I? This reaction is a confidence thing.

Growth   You can have all of the aforementioned qualities, yet no growth. Lack of growth would immediately remove such a company from my acceptance radar screen.

Going Short

Obviously, if I am looking for a stock to short, I would dearly like to see no earnings, no growth, a high P/E ratio, and very little insider ownership. A candidate for shorting should clearly lack a business model and possess a ton of fluff. Then, I look for overvaluation with the stock chart rolling over to the downside. The "dot-nothing" era of the new millennium is a good example of the type of stocks that I am looking to short. Many prices were based on nothing more than a wish and a promise, comprising absolutely no substance. Before you run out and short one of these puppies, check out the chart. These types of ridiculous valuations can persist for extended periods of time. You will be right, but do you need the pain? Of course, the answer is: no, you don't. To avoid that pain, look at the chart of the sector in which such a stock resides. Make sure that you have the weakest stock in the sector and that the chart is showing indications of a topping pattern, with what looks like a distribution. Also, look for thinning volume on the rallies, with heavier volume on the retreats. If the chart looks like a pole, don't try to guess how high that pole will go. Froth is not easily measured.

Once you have chosen your target, keep a close watch on it. As the stock rolls over to the downside, look for confirmations of that reversal of trend. That is a good point at which to sell the stock and to buy a cheap call, overhead. Don't forget to sell the puts that cover your short if the stock drops. Now you have a position that is hedged for the time until the options expire.

FUNDAMENTAL FILTERS DONE

Now we take the few remaining stocks on our list and start to review the charts. I look for trending stocks, either up or down, and stocks that are undervalued and cheap, forming a basing pattern. As an option seller, I have to be careful with the stocks that pay a dividend so that I get the dividend if I am long and I don't have to pay the dividend if I am short. As a short seller, one has a personal obligation to pay the dividend on the shorted stock. For example, if stock XYZ pays a $1.00 dividend and you are short the stock, your account will be debited for the dividend payment. It works this way: When you short a stock, you borrow somebody else's stock and sell it, trying to capture a decline in the price of that stock. As a borrower, you are responsible to make the lender whole regarding the return of the stock and the payment of all dividends.

USING TECHNICALS TO SOLVE FOR WHERE TO GO LONG OR SHORT

I have spent a great deal of time in this book talking about technical analysis. Here is the place where all the knowledge will come into play. Once you know what stock or issue you either like, hate, or believe will go nowhere, you are armed with half of the information that will be necessary to optimize your choice. Then is the time when you need to look at those charts. As you know, a chart is a picture of the action of the stock. On the chart you can easily see at which point selling seems to enter the market and at which point buying pops up to support the price. These two levels are important for you to find and understand. Of course, I haven't spoken about markets that are going sideways, and that observation needs to be noted as well. The charts are your road map. So, let us start with the buy, or going long.

Going Long

Before I do anything, I look for sectors that are leading the market. I am looking for those industries that are in the hot area for investing. In general, I will not run after hot sectors, but I like to look into these sectors, just to see who the leaders are. This is done in an effort to find other related industries that could become the next hot sector to consider. For example, let's say that you like housing. You would look at the financial institutions that provide the mortgages and make money on setting up these instruments. Then you might take a look at the insurers that will have to insure these properties, as well as the durable goods and home furnishings industries. Next you would look at stocks like Lowe's or Home Depot, which will enjoy sales from both the new and used home buyer. Get the picture?

After you find a group that you believe will prosper, look for the strongest company in that group. This stock will be the leader in the expected rally. Then, go through the filters I mentioned earlier. I look for growth, earnings from operations, good book value, good debt coverage, and (what I like) no pension liabilities. Then, I look for insider ownership. It is always nice the have the owners running the show. They tend to care more about the outcome and take pride in their company. Next, if the company has a risk to fuel, agriculture, or currencies, I like to see that it has hedging mechanisms in place to offset some of the possible risks in its market. For example, if it is an airline, I like to see that its fuel needs have been hedged in the futures markets. If it is an exporter, I like to know that its currency risk has been hedged.

As mentioned, once you have found these companies, you need to look at the charts. Here is where the fun begins. We are looking for stocks that are breaking out to the upside, or for stocks that have been forming a bottom and are getting ready to move to the upside. I use various technical tools to find my best candidates. It is really important to avoid penny stocks or stocks with a very small float and very limited volume. You certainly don't want to own all the shares or have a problem getting out of the stock when you decide to sell the issue.

First, I must thank Fred the garlic-eating broker at Thomson McKinnon for introducing me to a publication called *Value Line*. I have been a subscriber since early in the 1980s, when I discovered that the quality of information is important. This guy also read some other publications, but none as valuable as *Value Line*. It seems as though my life and attire have flipped 180 degrees. In the board room at TMcK it was appropriate to wear suits and look really businesslike. On the floor a suit would be questionable attire bringing questions about possible funerals, weddings, or something else important enough to dress up for.

A thought hit me that fundamental analysis was very much akin to wearing suits in the board rooms. Fundamentalists speak with suits sitting in offices at the companies being researched. The suits depend on suits for their information about the company. It is a rather clean and formal way of doing business and research. The technical analyst gets down and dirty and moves into the trade without the need of a formal suit, nor does he need any information from the company about options, inventory, or anything else. He is the guy with ink on his shirt, pencils hanging out of his pockets, a calculator, and probably a pocket protector. Yes, we are nerds; somebody has to be a nerd and fess up to it. We take the demonstrable behavior of the stock, plot it on a chart, and voilà: a subject worthy of study is produced. We review the data and study the actions and reactions of the security and then and only then make judgments on that security.

I remember many long hours going through the blue *Daily Graphs* chart book and the green *Daily Graphs* chart book looking for possible buy or sell candidates. No matter where you start, either with fundamentals or with technicals, you have to begin the process or that process is one of elimination. For shorts, you are looking for the worst stock in the market and for the longs you are looking for the best-looking company in the market. In either case, you are looking for outperformance potential for the future trade.

STOCKS VERSUS BONDS VERSUS COMMODITIES

Equities pose a greater challenge than do commodities or bonds. Why? Because there are many more variables in there that must be adjusted. True, commodities and bonds have their own problems but they seem to have fewer variables and outside constraints that can affect your analysis. When looking for and finding equities in which to invest, you must view the economy, the global effects on that economy, the markets, the currency, the sector and its relationship to the overall market, and then the stock or exchange-traded fund (ETF) if that is your choice. For a bond, you look at the ability of the borrower to pay the loan, what hard assets back that loan, the call feature on that loan, the indenture's language, and the ratings of that bond. Further, you look at the convexity and duration of the bond. You review the economic climate for interest rate increases and the income flow on which the promised payment of interest and principal are made. (This is a brief overview.) For commodities, you look at the economy, the weather for agricultural commodities, global growth for energies, inflation for precious metals, economic growth for industrial metals, and so on. Again a very simplistic overview.

Obviously, I believe commodities are easier to read chartwise because there is less noise in the data. Not only that, most commodity traders and managers are closet technicians. The charts are clean. If you are looking at coffee, you are looking at a pattern, with clear support and resistance levels. The charts are easy to read. While we are captives of other markets and react to intermarket stresses and relationships, the ability to understand these factors and install them in the analysis is simple. For example, a cocoa trade will react if the U.S. dollar is strong and the pound sterling is weak; it makes sense that the market will be sold in New York and bought in London. The contracts offer an arbitrage opportunity that many traders take advantage of. Say the market in New York cocoa is strong and the U.S. dollar is strong; we have to believe that there is something to the rally in cocoa. The charts are easy to plot, with support and resistance levels that are easily found.

As you know by now, I work at the New York Board of Trade and have been known to trade most of the commodities traded on our floor. I seem to always return to my roots, the Russell indexes and options. One of the brightest traders calls our group and the whole floor community "the land of misfit toys," and indeed we are. I look around the ring and I see people who would never fit in any office. Most traders probably don't sit well and well, talk about aggressive! We are all A type personalities. My kids have frequently warned people, "Don't give Mom coffee, whatever you do! You think she is hyper now. Just wait." I guess we have high energy levels. To tell you the truth, I have never needed a sleeping pill. We have the nervous options traders, the local gentleman traders, the kids fresh out of college, some who never made it to college, lawyers, and even a plastic surgeon here. We dress as though we were going out to play, although I guess you would say that we *are* playing. The place is a zoo. Our alphas tell a tale without needing to say much. I traded with DDAY, HEF, GELT, JKR (we call him Joker), HORN, SID, FISH, WOO (Wally woo woo), MBA (can drink anybody anywhere under the table), MINI (would you believe he is vertically challenged or he thinks so), WHTY (about 6 foot 4 inches and blond), DRK, JOJO, WSA, SEA, ICY, UCHG, TPK, APL (we called him apple), FXIT (guess what he is great at), BARK, YME, USMC (a Marine to the core), and I am not making any of these alphas up. My alpha is GERT; that was my mother's name (actually Gerta). I am called YoGERT. The alpha is the letter combination you are allowed on your trading badge. How can we compare this world with that of the upstairs suits? Well, we can't. It is a world unto itself, a dying breed in the new world of electronic trading. One regret is that I know this world will one day disappear. It was a lot of fun while it lasted. I know, if it goes, I will miss it.

Then there was Roby, a Czech gentleman who had his favorite stocks. He was interesting and a very intelligent broker, but his motivation was ulterior and not to help me with sales, so I avoided that one. How could I not tell you about the Fox, a "big producer" broker who showed up at about noon daily to work. Foxy was married to Bootsy and his stock was Chief. That was oil and gas, and since I had no understanding of that I didn't accept that recommendation. The firm was pushing Damson Oil and Gas and Petro Lewis, but I avoided limited partnerships, which I didn't understand. It was the time of private placements and accruing interest payments that weren't made so that aggressive tax losses could be captured.

Back to stock selection. It dawned on me fairly quickly that I would have to find a way to ferret out good stocks in which to invest. Obviously, I couldn't rely on the other brokers to help me. I must say some of the best advice came to me via the other female broker on the floor. Rita always did her homework and did have some very interesting stock picks that seemed to work.

By now you probably have a list of about 12 issues that have been culled from a list of about 2,500. Twelve to about 20 issues will survive my filters, and after I am done only about four or five will remain. This process yields a great crop of stocks to invest in. As you go through these filters, you become familiar with the names that pop up all the time, so your reading is less difficult as you go on. I'll find some issues that technically are not in a good place for me to have an interest in today, but that will be very interesting in the future; I make a list of those stocks that are likely to be of later interest, if not today.

I am frequently called on by the media and given just a couple of hours in which to suggest some stocks in sectors that they have chosen. This requires a precommitted exercise in reading and studying for many hours. *Forbes on Fox*, thankfully, gives me at least a day to submit my stocks lists; of course, they choose the sectors. I submit at least three stocks from which they pick the ones that they like. This process is much like my process of picking out stocks to buy, except that I will be broadcasting my ideas rather than personally investing in them. Many companies have heard from this really stressed-out person asking rude questions about hedging and pension obligations. That person is me preparing for the program. Mind you, I have already looked at the stock on the charts, reviewed every piece of data I can find on the company on the company web page and the Internet. Still, I usually have questions that aren't answered, so they get the phone call. I usually avoid picking stocks for the telecast in which I have a position, because of the obvious legal complications. Several days after the broadcast, I am free to purchase these securities.

I look for stocks using technical analysis and the indicators described earlier, as well as uptrend lines, downtrend lines, and other technical tools available to me. With stocks that are breaking out to the upside, I like to measure where they will likely have future problems. If it is a new high, there will be no overhead resistance. I frequently use horizontal lines to find areas of congestion. These areas will offer either support or resistance. Resistance levels are seen as levels where the old investors are finally even on the trade so they sell the stock before another selling spree occurs. That is a level that can be found by looking on the chart for a band of previous trades at that level.

I frequently use weekly charts to find these issues. When I find a resistance area, one that I believe will cap the market, I sell calls at that level. Similarly, where I find support areas by using those same type of horizontal lines, I buy a put. Why? If the stock trades below that level, other sell orders (such as stop-loss orders) will be resting there and I don't want to be long that issue below that level.

Going Short

It is fairly clear that if I like earnings for stocks that I would like to buy, I don't want to see earnings in a stock that I am looking at as a possible short. Pension liabilities, in arrears, are great, along with lean to no earnings and high debt. Every factor that is important for me to consider in the purchase in a stock is the exact opposite of what I require in a possible short. Here, I would love to see a declining trend, with a breaking of a previous low support zone. Frankly, I must admit I am more likely to short an index than to short a single stock. Primarily, it is easier to get into and get out of and, secondly, I don't have to ask permission to short the issue. Further, I don't have to wait for an uptick to short, nor do I have to pay dividends.

FUTURES

Clearly, you can't look at an earnings report or at insider behavior on futures. You do have other things to think about, such as crop reports, hurricanes, droughts, or bird flu. For example, after and indeed during the 2006 hurricane season the price of frozen concentrated orange juice (FCOJ) rallied from about 88 cents to a high of 1.65. No, this did not happen as suddenly as it sounds. We had the first rally from 88 cents to about 1.07, then a retreat to about 94 cents, and then another rally to about 1.12, and so on. All of these events occurred as growers assessed the damage done to the crops and further to the trunks and root systems of the trees. Outside forces do play a role in either the cost increases or cost decreases, but technicals are easy to read. The coffee market trades at the end of

May and in early June as though, there could be a frost at any time in Brazil. The market worries that should there be a frost (there hasn't been one in Brazil since 2000), the supplies of coffee will be negatively impacted and thus the price will appreciate. Oil is another market that is impacted by news. But, in all these markets, the charts will show you the information you need to trade on. Even the run in FCOJ was tradable from a technical point of view. There were pullbacks and advances that could have been used for going either long or short.

As a technical analyst, I do pay some attention to these factors, but in truth very little attention. I have found that futures chart beautifully. While I would like to believe that my work is special, it really isn't all that unique; so I must believe that many of us are using similar information to arrive at the same conclusions. For example, many of us use pivot numbers with futures contracts. This is how we calculate them: we average high, low, open, and close; that becomes your pivot number. Then, to find for resistance 1, we take the pivot number and add to that the difference between the high of the period and the close. To solve for resistance 2, we take the pivot and add to it the difference between the high and the low. To solve for the support, we take the pivot and remove the difference between the low and the close, and then to solve for support 2, we take the pivot and remove the difference between the high and the low. Most traders do this for daily numbers, but I prefer to use 60-minute numbers.

I use uptrend lines and downtrend lines, drawing channels to help me further to find buy points and sell points. I also use an exponential five-period moving average as a trigger for very short trades. If you're above that number, you are long; below that number, short. Further, I calculate the Bollinger bands to show me when the market is at excess levels and as a guide to the volatility of the contract. I try to keep my work simple for quick trades. There is no way around it; I use weekly charts and monthly charts to help me make longer-term decisions. Sometimes, because I need more data, I will use the chart of the cash index. (The cash index is not a futures contract but rather is what the index is worth today this second in time if all the components were totaled.) For example, we have the S&P 500 cash and the S&P 500 December futures contract. The futures contract must calculate the cost of money and other variables that place it at a premium to today's value. (It's a premium in today's interest rate environment, but a few years ago it was a deficit because interest rates were so low; it became a negative number.) Once these calculations have been made, options that would complement my position are added. I also use the help of market profile charts. My charting page is always showing the same index in different time frames, along with information like advancing and declining issues, the VIX, and a number of other indicators that I use for the financial indexes.

CONCLUSION

Fundamental analysis is useful for ferreting out good buy candidates from a very long list of issues. It is always technical analysis and intermarket analysis that help me in my decisions. This isn't rocket science, and the old adage "Keep it simple, stupid" often applies.

There is no free lunch in the investment industry. If you find one, it probably is illegal and should be avoided. Always do your homework; don't be afraid to call the companies that you are interested in. Do research; it is a fun project for the entire family. Set your children or friends into motion. This is a treasure hunt with a real treasure at the end, so go for it!

Trading Tools I Have Developed

This appendix contains tools I have developed, based on the work of others, to help me to trade. The wonder of volume, the velocity trading tool, and the Commodity Channel Index twist all work to help make my (and your) trades more profitable. These three twists on trading might just help you make a little extra pocket change. While my velocity trading tool is good only for day traders, the other two can be used in varying time frames.

THE WONDER OF VOLUME

The "daily net change" indicator originated with a study of volume; its original intent was to be used in imputing volume into point and figure charts. I had planned to use color as an indication of sizable volume changes of the Xs and Os at that price. I was hoping that I could show visually the radical changes in the volume by using red for decreases in average volume and green for increases in average volume to bring attention to this deviation. As this study progressed, a new twist emerged, that is, volume relative to the size and extent of the move of the issue. Both Joseph Granville and Marc Chaikin have done some very important work on volume. In his 1963 book *Granville's New Key to Stock Market Profits* (Prentice Hall), Granville explored the on balance volume (OBV) indicator. In *Technical Analysis from A to Z*, 2nd Edition (McGraw-Hill, 2000), Marc Chaikin uses volume accumulation (VA) (in an indicator that he devised called Volume Accumulation Oscillator), which is more sensitive to intraday volume. Actually his study is similar to this one. Chaikin counts a percentage of the volume as a plus or minus using a daily mean. A percentage of the day's volume is given either a positive (if the issue is above the mean) or a negative (if the stock price is below the mean) number. These volumes are charted.

The formula is:

$$VA = \frac{(C - L) - (H - C)}{H - L} \times V$$

where C = close
L = low
H = high
V = volume

Richard Arms Jr. incorporates volume on bar charts to visually disclose the size of the move. The thinner the bar is, the lower the volume was that period. The fatter the bar, the heavier the volume for the period. This is easy to see but for charting these fat bars get in the way of your trend lines. With candles the equi-candle makes line drawing difficult.

Among the most important indicators an analyst can have is volume. "Volume goes with the trend" was an observation by Robert D. Edwards and John Magee in *Technical Analysis of Stock Trends* (Stock Trend Service, 1948, p. 24). Those words, often spoken but frequently misunderstood, are the colloquial expression for the general truth that trading activity tends to expand as prices move in the direction of the prevailing primary trend. Volume is a measurement of direct commitment. The probability of correct projections will be increased with the combination of price and volume.

J. Peter Steidlmayer feels that heavy volume indicates a balance in the market. He uses volume in his market profile system Market Profile and Short Form Capflow System at www.steidlmayer.com: "Volume is going to play a much more expanded role than in the past as our means of directional determination allows it to further describe this important focus."

Daily net change may be of interest to any equity buyer. It is a visual measurement of sincerity of the price change in an issue. This indicator cannot be used in the futures markets because volume is not always available on a timely basis. If volume were made available quickly, this indicator could be used. It is anticipated that buys and or sells can be generated in nontrending markets. Most other indicators need trending markets for effectiveness, but this one does not. According to *Volume Cycles in the*

Stock Market: Market Timing Through Equivolume Charting by Richard W. Arms Jr. (Equis International, 1994, p. 1), "We are interested in knowing the points at which . . . supply is overcoming demand and forcing prices downward. Price and volume figures can relay this information."

Daily net change is a measurement of the shareholders' commitment either into or out of the issue. The change in an issue's value is directly influenced by shareholder commitment. The daily net change quantifies that influence.

Net = Change in price from one bar ago (this will be a plus or minus number).

Average volume = Average volume for the past 60 days.

Percent change = In percent format the percent ± more or less than the average volume.

Daily net change = (+/–Net) × (+/– percent change in the issue)

This number is plotted above or below the zero line:

- Buy when the number becomes more positive.
- Sell when the number becomes more negative.

What this measurement is trying to find are the rallies or sell-offs that are on light volume. It is thought that a rally on light volume is not going to have much follow-through or value, just as a sell-off on light volume might lead to a reversal. This is what we are looking for:

- If the volume is negative and the price move is positive, the move will be a negative move.
- If the volume is positive and the price move is positive, the move will be positive.
- If the volume is positive and the price move is negative, the move will be negative.
- If the volume is negative and the price move is negative, the move will be positive.

VELOCITY TRADING TOOL

I have discovered that for scalping purposes during day trading, if I compute the rate of change (ROC) or the velocity of an issue, I can, with a fair degree of certainty, calculate how far above the high, or below the low, that issue is going to go. I am calculating the elasticity of the move. Stops tend to be both above and below the markets. These stops are, for the most part, market if touched (MIT) stops. In other words, should that price print, then the order becomes a market order. Many traders use these stops to get out of a bad short or to get out of a bad long. The order says that if a new low or high is printed for the day, then I want to get out of my position quickly. By calculating the ROC, I can see how far that MIT order is going to carry the market.

What I do is to calculate that number and then put on a trade, not joining but rather going in the opposite direction. I am trying to remove just a point or two in a quick trade. This works some 90 percent of the time, but there is that 10 percent of the time when you'll get mowed down by the market. This method works well with both the upper end and the lower end of the range. The order takes advantage of the emotional response to either a rally or a sell-off.

Here is an example: Say the market made a new high of 1,290 in the S&P 500 futures contract. Depending on the velocity of the rally, I would put in a sell order above that level. Why? Because as the shorts cover an artificial rally occurs, which is rectified as soon as the shorts have completed their covering. At that point, the market exhales and retreats. It is that retreat that I wish to take advantage of. This technique works as well on the downside; remember, you must calculate the velocity of that trade so as to find a spot to place your order.

COMMODITY CHANNEL INDEX TWIST

There is yet another tool of mine that I regularly use (mentioned in Chapter 5). It combines two existing indicators. I use the Commodity Channel Index (CCI), which was designed by Donald Lambert, in combination with a five-period exponential moving average. Why? Because the CCI, as conceived, is largely inefficient in getting you into or out of the market. It keeps you in the market longer or keeps you short longer. I had to develop a way to make this work for me, so what I did was place a five-period exponential moving average over the CCI, then use that crossover as a trigger to go either long or short. It works well and, in combination with some other indicators, has helped in trading.

Index

Abandoned options, 117
Accrued interest, on bonds, 97–98
Anchor charts, 26
Arbitrageur, 105, 167
Arms, Richard, Jr., 5, 208–209
Assigned options, 117
Automatic trading card (ATC),
31

Backing and filling. *See*
Consolidation periods
Backspreads, 160–162, 190
Back-testing, 16
Backwardation, 105
Bar charts, 7–10, 24–25
Bear Brothers, 44–47
Bear flag pattern, 77, 78
Beyond Candlesticks (Nison), 26,
36, 38
Black-Scholes option pricing
model, 121
Black shoe, in renko chart, 38
Bollinger bands, 87–88, 89
Bonds, 91–100, 106
call feature of, 114–115
maturation of, 95–97
put feature of, 115
stocks and commodities
contrasted to, 200–203

swaps of, 94
types of, 92–95
Box, 173
Breakaway gaps, 70–72
Bull flag pattern, 76–77
Butterflies, 139–147

Calendar spreads, 174–175
Callable bonds, 95–96, 114–115
Caller, in trading ring, 11
Calls, 110–114
Candlestick charts, 26–30
Cannonballing, 177
Certificates for amortizing
revolving debts (CARDs), 93
Certificates for automobile
receivables (CARs), 93
Chaikin, Marc, 207–208
Channel lines, 68–69
Charging, in trading ring, 11–12
Charts, 19–42
anchor charts, 26
bar charts, 7–10, 24–25
candlestick charts, 26–30
commodities and, 201
construction of basic, 6–10
equivolume charts, 41
futures and, 203
kagi charts, 36, 38

Charts (*Continued*)
  line charts, 9, 20–24
  market profile charts, 30–32
  point and figure charts, 5, 6, 33, 36–37
  renko charts, 38, 39
  three-line break charts, 38–40
  volume charts, 40
Collars, 124–125
Commodities, 91, 102–106. *See also* Futures
  stocks and bonds contrasted to, 200–203
Commodity Channel Index (CCI), 89, 210
Commodity trading adviser (CTA), 105
Computers, drawbacks of using, 16
Condors, 147–150
Consolidation periods, 47, 49, 51, 76
  identifying on charts, 55
Contango, 105
Contrarian traders, 44
Conversions, 124–125
Convertible bonds, 99–100, 128
Convertible preferred bonds, 100
Coupon bonds, 93–94
Covered calls, 111–113, 122, 190–192
Covered puts, 122
Credit spread, 137
Crossover moving averages, 86–87
Cumulative preferred bonds, 100
Currencies, 91, 101–102, 106
Currency pairs, 101

Daily Graphs chart, 200
Daily line charts, 20

Daily net change indicator, 207–209
Debit spread, 137
Delta, 130–131, 133
DeMark, Thomas, 88
Derivatives, options as, 109
Discount bonds, 94
Dividends, capturing while selling options, 124–125
Doji candlesticks, 28–30
Dollar-denominated bonds, 92–93
Double gap rule, 72
Dow Jones Industrial Average, 52
Dragonfly doji candlesticks, 30
Duration, of bonds, 96–97

Earnings, 196–197
Edwards, Robert D., 13–14, 208
Electronic trading, 52–53
Equivolume charts, 41
Exercise price, 116
Exhaustion gap, 72
Expiration date, 116–117
Expire worthless, defined, 117

Fabozzi, Frank J., 91, 96
Fan patterns, 59–63
Fibonacci, Leonardo, 64
Fibonacci arcs, 67–68
Fibonacci fans, 68
Fibonacci retracements, 64–67
Fifteen-minute charts, 22, 23
Five-minute charts, 22, 23
Flags, 75–79, 82
Floating rate bonds, 97
Floating stops, 190
Floor Committee, in trading ring, 12
Forbes on Fox, 202
Foreign bonds, 95
Foreign options, 125–127, 157–158

Fund, defined, 105
Fundamental analysis:
  technical analysis contrasted to, 13–17
  using, 196–198
Future behavior, predicting from patterns of past behavior, 7
Futures, 115–116, 203–204. *See also* Commodities
  traders of, 44–47
  vocabulary of, 105–106

Gamma, 130, 131, 133–134
Gap patterns, 70–72, 82
Good till canceled (GTC) orders, 185
Granville, Joseph, 207
Granville's New Key to Stock Market Profits (Granville), 207
Gravestone doji candlesticks, 29–30
Greeks, risk removal in trending markets, 130–136
Growth, 196–197

Handbook of Fixed Income Securities, The (Fabozzi), 91, 96
Head-and-shoulders tops and bottoms, 72–74, 82
Hedger, 105, 167
Hedging strategies, 123–124, 167–175
  box, 173
  calendar spreads, 174–175
  hedged trade, 170–171
  iron butterfly, 173
  simple trade, 169–170
  straddles, 125, 171–172
  strangles, 172–173
  vertical spread, 174
  wings, 150, 173–174

Historic volatility, 118
Human behavior, technical analysis as study of, 14–15

Implied volatility, 118
Indicators, 83–89
  Bollinger bands, 87–88, 89
  linearly weighted and exponential moving averages, 86–87
  relative strength index and stochastics, 83, 88–89
  simple moving averages, 83–85
Inflation, fixed income securities and, 97
Inside day, 81, 82
Insider ownership, 196–197
Insurance, on bonds, 95
Intermediate trends, 47, 48–49
International bonds, 92–93
In-the-money options, 117
Intraday charts, 9
Intraday trends, 47, 49
Intrinsic value, of options, 117
Iron butterfly, 173

Journal of the American Statistical Association, 7

Kagi charts, 36, 38

Lane, George, 88
Limit moves, 106
Linearly weighted and exponential moving averages, 86–87
Line charts, 9, 20–24
Locals, in trading ring, 11, 105
Log scales, 25
Long day candlesticks, 28
Long futures, 103–105

Long positions:
   fundamental analysis and,
      196–197
   managing winning, 190–192
   repairing with options, 183–184
   technical analysis and,
      198–200
Losing positions, managing,
      177–187
   futures contracts and, 178–183
   long position, 183–184
   short position, 184–187

Magee, John, 13–14, 208
M and W reversal patterns, 79–81,
      82
Mann, Steven M., 91
Margin, 103–104, 126–127
Market profile charts, 30–32
Mispriced options, 129
Momentum. *See* Indicators
Monthly charts, 9, 20, 21
Moving average
      convergence/divergence
      (MACD), 85, 86–87
Moving averages:
   linearly weighted and
      exponential, 86–87
   simple, 83–84
M pattern, 79–80
Municipal bonds, 98–99
Murphy, John, 68, 85

Naked calls, 121–122
Naked puts, 122
Neck, in renko chart, 38
Negative movement positions. *See*
   Reversing markets
Neutral positions. *See* Hedging
   strategies
*New Science of Technical
   Analysis, The* (DeMark), 88
Nison, Steve, 26, 36, 38

Non-dollar-denominated bonds,
      92–93
Notes:
   municipal, 99
   Treasury, 93

Open interest, 34, 104–105
Open outcry markets, 11
Options, 109–128
   basics of, 110, 127–128
   calls and puts explained,
      110–114
   combining purchases and sales,
      124–125
   as derivatives, 109
   European versus American,
      125–127
   uses of, 114–116, 123–124
   vocabulary of, 116–122
Out-of-the-money options,
      117
Outside day, 81

Packages, 151
Pairs trading, 167
Paper brokers, 11
Pattern recognition, 13, 59–82
   channel lines, 68–69
   fans, 59–63
   Fibonacci arcs, 67–68
   Fibonacci fans, 68
   Fibonacci retracements, 64–67
   flags, 75–79, 82
   gaps, 70–72, 82
   head-and-shoulders tops and
      bottoms, 72–74, 82
   inside and outside day, 82
   M and W reversal, 79–81, 82
   reversal day, 69–70
   rounding top, 76
   saucer bottom, 76, 82, 156
   teacup bottom, 76, 82
Pennant pattern, 7, 78

Pits. *See* Trading ring, life in
Point and figure charts, 5, 6, 33, 36–37
Premium bonds, 94
Premiums, 111, 118
Price, technical analysis of, 4, 5
Price-earnings ratio, 196–197
Price-sensitive charts, 32–41
Primary trends, 47, 48
Producer, defined, 105
Put packages, 158–160
Puts, 110–114
Puttable bonds, 96, 115

Range, 9
Range-bound markets, 139–152
   butterflies, 139–147
   condors, 147–150
   packages, 151
   trees, 150–151
   wings, 150
Ratio spreads, 136–137, 158–162
Relative strength index (RSI), 83, 88–89
Renko charts, 38, 39
Repurchase agreement (repo) bonds, 97
Resistance levels, 47–48, 54, 57
   breaks in, 56–57
   identifying on charts, 55
   moving averages and, 86
   supply and, 54
   time and, 56
   volume and, 55–56
Reversal patterns, 69–70, 79–81
Reverse repo bonds, 97
Reversing markets, 153–163
   commonsense trading rules, 154–156
   European versus American options and, 156–158

indicators of, 154
pricing multipliers and, 157
strategies for, 158–163
Rho, 133
Risk removal. *See* Hedging strategies
Rounding top patterns, 76
Runaway gap, 71, 72

Saucer bottom patterns, 76, 82, 156
Scalping, 43, 45
Secular trends, 48
Sentiment, technical analysis and, 5
Short day candlestick, 28
Short futures, 103–105
Short positions:
   fundamental analysis and, 197–198
   managing winning, 192–193
   repairing with options, 184–187
   technical analysis and, 198–200
Short-term trends, 47, 49
Sideways markets, 49–51
Simple moving averages, 83–85
Single bar charts, 7–10, 24, 25
Sinking fund bonds, 97
Sixty-minute charts, 22, 24
Spinning top candlestick, 28
Spur, in trading ring, 12
Stair-step trend patterns, 47, 48
Steidlmayer, J. Peter, 31
Stochastics, 83, 88–89
Stocks, bonds and commodities contrasted to, 200–203. *See also* Long positions; Short positions
Stop-loss orders, 52, 56, 60
Straddles, 125, 171–172
Strangles, 172–173
Strike price, 116

Support levels, 54, 57
  breaks in, 56–57
  buying and, 54–55
  moving averages and, 86
  time and, 56
  volume and, 55–56
Synthetics, 162–163, 173

Tax issues:
  discount bonds, 94
  futures, 104
  municipal bonds, 98–99
  Treasury notes and bonds,
    93–94
  zero coupon bonds, 94–95
Teacup bottom patterns, 76,
    82
Technical analysis, 3–17
  contrasted to fundamental
    analysis, 13–17
  information from charts and,
    6–10
  longs and shorts and, 198–200
  types of, 4–5
  uses of, 12–13
  variety of tools for, 10–12
  visual presentations and,
    3–4
Technical Analysis from A to Z
    (Chaikin), 207–208
*Technical Analysis of Stock
    Trends* (Edwards and Magee),
    13–14, 208
*Technical Analysis of the
    Financial Markets* (Murphy),
    85
*Technical Analysis of the Futures
    Markets* (Murphy), 68
Theoretical value, of option,
    121
Theta, 131–134
Three-box reversal, 36, 37
Three-line break charts, 38–40

Tick charts, 22
Tick value, 103
Time:
  calculating time value, 117–118
  support and resistance levels
    and, 56
  technical analysis and, 5
  trends and, 51–52
Time decay. *See* Theta
Time-sensitive charts, 19–31
Trade input personnel (TIPs)
    machine, 31
Trading ring, life in, 11–12, 34–35,
    46, 52–53, 66, 201–202
Trading tools, 207–210
Treasury notes and bonds, 93,
    103–104
Trees (options strategy for range-
    bound market), 150–151
Trending markets, 129–137
  Greeks and risk removal,
    130–136
  ratio spreads and, 136–137
Trends, 43–47, 57
  directions in, 49–51
  kinds and durations of,
    47–49
  revealed in charts, 4
  time and, 51–52
  tips for trading on, 52
  volume and, 51

Underlying instrument, defined,
    116
U.S. Dollar Index (USDX), 101

Value Line publications, 195,
    199
Vance, Ray, 7
Variable rate bonds, 97
Vega, 132–133
Velocity trading tool, 209–210
Vertical spread, 174

VIX (volatility measure), 5, 119–121
Volatility, 118–121
    Greeks and, 132–133
    measures of, 5
    winning position management
        and, 192
Volume:
    charts and, 40
    daily net change indicator and,
        207–209
    as indicator of market direction,
        154
    resistance levels and, 55–56
    technical analysis and, 4–5
    trends and, 51

Volume Cycles in the Stock Market
    (Arms), 208–209
VXN (volatility measure), 5

Wedge pattern, 79
Weekly charts, 9, 20, 21
Wilder, J. Welles, Jr., 88
Wings, 150, 173–174
Winning positions, managing,
    189–193
W pattern, 80–81

Yield bonds, 93–94

Zero coupon bonds, 94–95, 98